WEDDING DRESS
STYLE

WEDDING DRESS STYLE

Catherine Woram

THE INDISPENSABLE STYLE-FILE
FOR BRIDES-TO-BE AND DESIGNERS

THE
APPLE
PRESS

A QUINTET BOOK

Published by The Apple Press
6 Blundell Street
London, N7 9BH

ISBN 1–85076–463–8

This book was designed and produced by
Quintet Publishing Limited
6 Blundell Street
London N7 9BH

Creative Director: Richard Dewing
Designer: Chris Dymond
Project Editor: Stefanie Foster
Editor: Michelle Clark
Picture Researcher: Jill Anne De Cet

Typeset in Great Britain by
Central Southern Typesetters, Eastbourne
Manufactured in Hong Kong by
Regent Publishing Services Limited
Printed in Hong Kong by
Leefung-Asco Printers Limited

CONTENTS

INTRODUCTION

A WEDDING GOWN IS ARGUABLY THE SINGLE MOST IMPORTANT OUTFIT THAT A WOMAN WILL CHOOSE IN HER LIFE. IT IS ALSO LIKELY TO BE THE MOST EXPENSIVE AND, INDEED, GENERALLY THE BRIDE'S OUTFIT IS THE SINGLE MOST COSTLY ITEM ON A WEDDING LIST AFTER THE RECEPTION AND THE HONEYMOON, SO CHOOSING THE RIGHT WEDDING GOWN IS OF GREAT IMPORTANCE TO EVERY BRIDE.

▽ A PRINCESS LINE GOWN BY DESIGNER FIONA CLARE IS EMBELLISHED WITH GOLD BEADS AND PEARLS AROUND THE NECKLINE AND CUFFS. THE BRIDE WEARS AN ORNATE TIARA-STYLE HEAD-DRESS OF PEARLS AND BEADS, ECHOING THE DECORATION ON THE GOWN.

This book sets out to provide prospective brides, designers and dressmakers with a comprehensive source of ideas and inspiration for wedding gowns, accessories and outfits for the bridal attendants.

The myriad styles of wedding gown available to today's bride-to-be are at once exciting and daunting. The contemporary bride may plunder fashion history in the quest for her ideal gown, which could be anything from a Tudor-esque bodice with panniered skirt to a drop-waisted flapper's dress imitating those of the 1920s. Alternatively she may look to any one of the leading fashion designers to provide her ideal gown.

Each bride has her own particular needs and preferences that will, ultimately, determine her choice of wedding gown. Some brides-to-be picture themselves in a fairy-tale gown and they have nurtured this image in their minds since childhood; others, of a more practical nature, want for the dress to have what is usually called an after life, meaning that it can be worn again after the wedding; while yet others desire a dress that simply defies all conventional notions of the traditional, all-white wedding gown.

Reference is made throughout this book to the various period styles that influence contemporary bridalwear designs as well as other historical sources that might inspire the reader. It should be noted at this point that the book is intended to provide a source of ideas and inspiration rather than be a detailed history of costume and, thus, a certain amount of literary licence has been taken when describing specific styles. Just as the theatrical costumier may incorporate various bodices, sleeves and skirt styles from different decades of, say, the eighteenth century to convey a certain historical style, many of the descriptions contained within this book are perhaps more theatrical than historically accurate. This, however, is all part of the romance surrounding the wedding gown.

While the wedding dress itself is undoubtedly the most important consideration for any bride, her choice of outfits for the attendants also deserves careful thought and attention. It is the outfits for the bridesmaids, flower-girls, page-boys and matron of honour that set the mood or define the theme of the wedding itself. This in turn may influence the bride's choice of flowers, decorations for the church and reception as well as the style and decoration of the wedding cake.

◁ LORENZO RIVA'S WEDDING GOWN TYPIFIES THE RECENT TREND TOWARDS SIMPLICITY THAT APPEARS TO BE SHAPING BRIDALWEAR DESIGNS IN THE 1990S. THE PLAIN DRESS BODICE FEATURES A DUCHESSE SATIN SKIRT DECORATED WITH SIMPLE WHITE FLOWERS DOWN THE BACK.

The traditional white wedding gown remains the most popular choice among the majority of brides in the Western world. However, there are trends in wedding fashions that come and go, just as they do for other clothes. The choice of black or black and white gowns for older bridal attendants has enjoyed great popularity in America in the past few years, as the dramatic contrast of colours provides the perfect foil for the bride. More recently, many American brides have decided on a colour theme for the wedding party that ensures a harmonious setting for the wedding photographs. While this particular trend appears to be uniquely American, many other brides will recognize the potential problem of Aunt Agatha's turquoise picture hat clashing with her new mother-in-law's cerise pink suit, spoiling her photographs of the big day, so it is worth thinking about.

While this book cannot aspire to remedy this particular problem, it is hoped that it may provide every bride-to-be with ideas and inspiration for the most important day of her life.

▷ LORENZO RIVA'S SCULPTURED BRIDAL GOWN OF DUCHESSE SATIN EVOKES THE STYLE OF 1950S COUTURE. THE BODICE FEATURES A V-SHAPED NECKLINE AND RAGLAN SLEEVES, AND IS FITTED TO THE SKIRT WHICH FORMS DEEP-PLEATED PANELS. LAYERS OF TULLE WRAPPED AROUND THE SHOULDERS FORM A SHAWL.

1
SOURCES AND INSPIRATION

△ This Empire-style wedding gown of 1814, an early example of a white gown, is made of silk gauze and embroidered with white satin. The model wears loose satin gloves and a head-dress of white marguerites and orange blossom.

PAST AND PRESENT

TODAY'S BRIDE-TO-BE IS FACED WITH AN ALMOST LIMITLESS CHOICE OF DESIGNS, STYLES AND FABRICS AVAILABLE FOR HER WEDDING GOWN. IN THE PAST, MOST WEDDING GOWNS FOLLOWED THE PREVAILING FASHION OF THAT PARTICULAR PERIOD. FOR EXAMPLE, IN THE 1920S, BRIDAL OUTFITS CONSISTED OF TUBE OR CHEMISE DRESSES WITH THE LOW WAISTS TYPICAL OF THAT ERA; BRIDES OF THE EARLY 1950S OFTEN CHOSE TO WEAR SUITS WITH FITTED JACKETS FEATURING SLOPING SHOULDERS AND FULL CALF-LENGTH SKIRTS, REFLECTING CHRISTIAN DIOR'S NEW LOOK; MANY WEDDING DRESSES OF THE 1960S WERE SHORT, INFLUENCED BY THE FASHION FOR MINI SKIRTS.

Of course, such bridal gowns sometimes incorporated design influences from the past, too. It is said that the dress worn by Lady Elizabeth Bowes-Lyon (now the Queen Mother) at her marriage to the Duke of York in 1923 was inspired by an Italian medieval gown, although its shape reflected the tubular fashions of the 1920s.

WHY WHITE?

Although it is easy to imagine that the tradition of the white wedding gown is as old as the ceremony of marriage itself, it is, in fact, a product of the Victorian era. Queen Victoria established the trend with the gown she wore at her marriage to Prince Albert in February 1840. There are examples of white gowns before this date, but the wearing of white was not as predominant as it has been since then. Today, white is the most commonly-worn colour, although antique white, ivory and cream have become favourite alternatives over the past decade, indubitably as a result of the Princess of Wales' choice for her wedding gown, designed by the Emanuels in 1981. There are no hard and fast rules determining the colour of a wedding gown, although superstitious brides-to-be might heed the old verse:

Married in white, you have chosen right, Married in green, ashamed to be seen, Married in grey, you will go far away, Married in red, you will wish yourself dead, Married in blue, love ever true, Married in yellow, you're ashamed of your fellow, Married in black, you'll wish yourself back, Married in pink, of you he'll aye think.

From *And the Bride Wore . . .* by Ann Monserrat
(Gentry Books, London, 1973)

However, many brides ignore superstition and some have even opted to wear the fated red, including Paula Yates who wore an all-red gown with long train and veil and a head-dress of red roses at her marriage to rock singer Bob Geldof.

△ LADY DIANA SPENCER'S ROMANTIC WEDDING GOWN OF IVORY TAFFETA, DESIGNED BY THE EMANUELS IN 1981, HERALDED A REVIVAL OF THIS STYLE, WHICH WAS THE MOST POPULAR SHAPE FOR A GREAT PART OF THE 1980S AND IS STILL THE FIRST CHOICE OF MANY BRIDES.

◁ THE LOW-WAISTED GOWNS OF THE 1920S CONTINUE TO BE A FAVOURITE CHOICE FOR MANY PROSPECTIVE BRIDES. THIS GOWN BY CATHERINE BUCKLEY FEATURES A BEADED CHIFFON TABARD THAT HANGS FROM THE SHOULDERS. THE BRIDAL HEAD-DRESS, WORN LOW ON THE FOREHEAD, IS TYPICAL OF THE STYLE OF THIS PERIOD.

△ PAULA YATES CHOSE TO WEAR RED FOR HER MARRIAGE TO ROCK STAR BOB GELDOF. THE ROMANTIC-STYLE GOWN WAS CREATED FOR HER BY BRITISH DESIGNER JASPER CONRAN, COMPLETE WITH A RED VEIL.

◁ THIS ROMANTIC-STYLE WEDDING GOWN IN IVORY SILK, DESIGNED BY JENNY BURGESS, FEATURES A LONG TRAIN AND IS DECORATED WITH ELABORATE SILK ROSES. THE BRIDE WEARS A LARGE STRAW HAT, WREATHED WITH MATCHING SILK FLOWERS.

12

▽ A DRESS WORN AS A WEDDING GOWN
NEED NOT HAVE BEEN DESIGNED
SPECIFICALLY FOR THAT PURPOSE TO BE
SUCCESSFUL – MANY BRIDES FIND THEIR
IDEAL DRESS IN THE GENERAL
COLLECTIONS OF A FAVOURITE
DESIGNER. FOR EXAMPLE, GIANNI
VERSACE'S FULL-SKIRTED GOWN
EMBELLISHED WITH HEAVY GOLD LACE
COULD BE WORN AS A SHORT WEDDING
DRESS EVEN THOUGH IT IS NOT LABELLED
AS SUCH.

△ LORENZO RIVA'S DELICATE LACE
BRIDAL GOWN FEATURES A STRAPLESS
DRESS WITH A SHORT, FULL SKIRT, WORN
BENEATH A MATCHING COAT OF SHEER
LACE, FEATURING A TRAIN. THE BRIDE
CARRIES A SIMPLE SHEAF OF WHITE
TULIPS BOUND WITH SATIN RIBBON.

Where to find the ideal gown

Specialist shops and departments in big stores

There are many ways of choosing a wedding gown. Bridal boutiques and departments within large stores sell off-the-peg designs by a variety of well-known designers and manufacturers in different price ranges. These gowns are ready-made and will usually be altered as necessary by the shop or boutique, although the alterations they will do are often minor, such as hem lengths or bodice adjustments. Many bridal boutiques will also undertake to provide the outfits for the attendants as well as the bride's accessories, such as the veil and head-dress, gloves, bag and shoes. By offering a complete "bridal package", these stores and boutiques can help brides decide on an overall theme or style that can be carried right through to the last detail of her own outfit and those of her attendants.

Shows and exhibitions

Catwalk shows, hosted by large department stores, and bridal exhibitions, organized by specialist companies (often in conjunction with a national bridal magazine), are a good way of seeing a variety of gowns by different designers at one visit. Bridal exhibitions usually feature companies specializing in everything from photography to caterers as well as outfits for the bride, groom and attendants. The ever-increasing number of small companies offering a host of specialist bridal services usually advertise in the classified sections of bridal magazines. These range from lace and beaded motifs with which to customize a wedding gown and shoes, to embroidered ringbearer cushions and silk-covered prayer books.

Bridal designers

A made-to-measure dress can be created by bridal designers whose businesses range from the smallest studios specializing in exclusive

△ THE WEDDING GOWN BY DESIGNER HELEN MORLEY FEATURES A HEAVY GUIPURE LACE BODICE AND SLEEVES WHILE THE CIRCULAR, SUNRAY PLEATED SKIRT IS OF SHEER SILK GEORGETTE. THE BODICE IS FASTENED DOWN THE BACK WITH TINY COVERED BUTTONS.

one-off designs to large-scale salons producing hundreds of gowns each month. Most designers are recognized for having their own house style. While they are usually happy to accommodate a customer's own style preferences, it is obviously preferable to go to a designer whose particular style of design suits a bride's tastes. For example, if a bride wants a slim-fitting sheath dress, it is better for her to choose a designer who creates such gowns, rather than one who specializes in traditional, full-blown romantic styles.

Recommendation by word of mouth is always a good way of finding out about designers, particularly young up-and-coming names who operate small businesses and are unable to afford to advertise widely. The many bridal magazines and wedding guides available also provide a good guide to current trends as well as covering a wide selection of designers and manufacturers, complete with price guides.

DRESSMAKERS

For those brides who have a specific style in mind for their gown, perhaps having designed it themselves or seen a design they like in a book or magazine, a seamstress or dressmaker should be able to interpret it. Alternatively, paper patterns available from the big dressmaking pattern companies come in a wide variety of styles and these can be made up by a dressmaker in the bride's choice of fabric and trimmings. There are also many patterns available for the bride's attendants, from young flower-girls and page-boys to grown-up brides-maids and matrons of honour. It is worth while remembering, too, that many designs outside of the bridal section of pattern catalogues can make ideal outfits, made up in appropriate fabrics.

▽ A SLENDER, FIGURE-SKIMMING GOWN IS AN ELEGANT ALTERNATIVE TO THE FULL- BLOWN ROMANTIC GOWN. THE SILK DUPION GOWN BY RONALD JOYCE HERE FEATURES LONG SLEEVES WITH TINY COVERED SILK BUTTONS AND CORNELLI EMBROIDERY ON THE BODICE. THE DRESS PANELS FLARE OUT TOWARDS THE HEM TO FORM A LONG TRAIN.

ANTIQUE AND OTHER SHOPS
. . . .

Another good source for prospective brides looking for an unusual gown or an authentic example of a period style are antique or second-hand clothing stalls in markets, thrift shops and even auctions. While the thought of wearing an old dress may not appeal to everyone, there are beautiful examples of handwork to be found in such places. Handmade lace, intricate beadwork and unusual fabrics are features that are worth looking out for. It is also worth while remembering that, although a second-hand 1920s beaded gown may appear expensive, to reproduce it at today's prices would be prohibitive – even if you could find someone to do it.

Edwardian and Victorian handmade lace garments and trimmings can be incorporated into a new gown. An antique lace blouse, for example, creates a ready-made bodice, to which can be added a skirt in similar or contrasting fabric. Antique lace petticoats can be layered together and fitted with a new bodice and sleeves to make dresses for flower-girls, finished with a wide satin sash tied around the waist in a bow. Antique garments and pieces of lace that have been passed down through the family can be "borrowed", either for the bridal gown or attendants' outfits, thus incorporating two requirements of the old proverb that states "Something *old*, something new, something *borrowed*, something blue".

It is always wise to exercise care when buying antique or second-hand garments. Alterations to heavily beaded garments, for instance, are generally expensive, as can be the replacement of missing beads. As long as lace and cotton is not heavily stained, it usually cleans well after soaking it in a gentle detergent, and starch will give a crisp finish, but other marks may be harder or even impossible to remove, so garments need to be carefully checked before buying.

◁ THEATRICAL COSTUMIERS CAN BE A GOOD SOURCE FOR UNUSUAL WEDDING GOWNS. HEAVY DUCHESSE SATIN IS USED TO CREATE THIS GOWN WITH AN EMBROIDERED BODICE FROM ANGEL & BERMANS.

FANCY DRESS SHOPS AND THEATRICAL COSTUMIERS

For a more unusual bridal gown, many fancy dress shops and theatrical costumiers hire out gowns in a great variety of period styles, from lavish eighteenth-century costumes to slinky 1930s gowns inspired by the Hollywood movie stars of those years. Such places are also a good source for attendants' clothes, from velvet "Little Lord Fauntleroy" outfits with lace collars and cuffs and sailor suits for page-boys to original ballerina tutus for flower-girls. The state of such costumes obviously depends on how many times they have been hired out and worn, but a good drycleaner should be able to restore them to their former glory.

BRIDALWEAR HIRE SHOPS

The growing number of bridalwear hire shops are a good option for the bride who cannot afford to buy the dress of her dreams. A designer-label gown can be hired for the day at a significantly lower price than it would cost to buy. Although this means that the dress is the bride's for only a day, many prefer to hire a top-quality gown than buy a cheaper one. Prices for hiring bridal gowns vary, depending on its original cost as well as its condition (those that have been worn several times are less expensive to hire.)

FASHION HOUSES

In the quest for the ideal dress, it is also worth remembering that many fashion designers produce outfits in their mainstream collections that are eminently suitable for a wedding. If a bride has a favourite fashion designer whose clothes have always made her feel good, an evening gown or perhaps a suit by that designer could prove the perfect choice.

An *haute couture* gown, especially with a Paris label, has long been considered to be the *crème de la crème* of wedding gowns. The rest of the fashion world still looks towards Paris – where the long-established names in *haute couture* have always resided – as the centre of creativity and inspiration. Chapter 5, Fashionable Brides, provides a glimpse into the world of *haute couture*.

△ THE LITTLE LORD FAUNTLEROY OUTFIT FROM ANGEL & BERMANS IS A POPULAR STYLE FOR PAGE-BOYS AND CAN BE BOUGHT FROM BRIDAL SHOPS, HIRED FROM THEATRICAL COSTUMIERS OR FANCY DRESS SHOPS. THE BLACK VELVET SUIT FEATURES SILVER BUTTONS AND AN ORNATE LACE COLLAR.

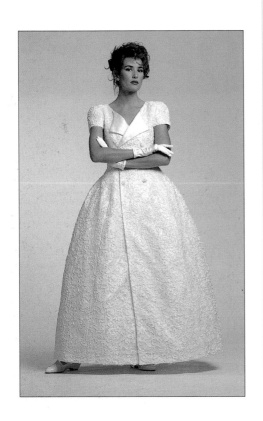

△ LUCIANA DE STEFANO'S
SOPHISTICATED TAILORED GOWN IS
DOUBLE-BREASTED AND FEATURES SATIN
LAPELS WHILE THE SHORT SLEEVES HAVE
LIGHTLY PADDED AND SHAPED
SHOULDERS.

△ AN EXTRAVAGANT EIGHTEENTH-
CENTURY-STYLE BODICE BY COUTURIER
CHRISTIAN LACROIX FEATURES
DETACHABLE SLEEVES AND HEAVY GILT
MOTIFS. THE BRIDE WEARS AN ORNATE
OVAL- SHAPED VEIL OF LACE.
© Niall McInerney

◁ DEBORAH MILNER'S LUSTROUS SATIN
WEDDING COAT IS INSPIRED BY THE
COSTUMES OF THE ELIZABETHAN PERIOD.
THE HIGH STANDAWAY COLLAR IS EDGED
WITH HEAVY LACE, REMINISCENT OF THE
ELABORATE RUFFS OF ELIZABETHAN
DRESS.

△ WEDDING GOWNS CAN BE AS
CLASSICAL OR AS AVANT-GARDE AS
PERSONAL TASTE DICTATES. PAM HOGG'S
FUR-TRIMMED MINIDRESS IN OFF-WHITE
SATIN IS WORN WITH A DEEP-CROWNED
HAT IN PLACE OF THE TRADITIONAL NET
VEIL.

▽ A DELICATE BRIDAL HEADPIECE
ADORNED WITH SEA SHELLS WOULD MAKE
A PERFECT HEAD-DRESS FOR A TROPICAL
WEDDING OUTFIT. DESIGNED BY
CECILIA, THIS HAIR ORNAMENT
FEATURES SPIRAL-SHAPED SHELLS,
PEARLS AND TINY FLOWERS.

THINKING ABOUT ACCESSORIES

The wedding gown is only part of a complete bridal outfit and therefore it is vital to envisage the complete look before setting out to choose accessories. Helen Fifield, publisher of the British bridal magazine *Brides & Setting Up Home*, maintains that "brides often spend a lot of money on their wedding dresses and then don't have any money left for shoes. I think it is important to think the look all the way through and *not* skimp on accessories, which are just as important. In fact, you can have the plainest dress with a wonderful bouquet of flowers and an amazing head-dress that will completely lift the whole outfit". On the other side of the Atlantic, American Editor-in-Chief of *Brides & Your New Home* adds that "People are more accessory-conscious today and when they get married that interest gets carried over".

THE HEAD-DRESS

The head-dress – whether it be a traditional veil, hat or floral creation – is certainly an important item to consider and it is worth bearing in mind the kind of head-dress preferred when deciding upon the gown. There are no set rules regarding bridal head-dresses, but there are certain styles that are associated with different gowns because they look right with those shapes and proportions. There is no reason why a 1920s-style cloche hat should not be worn with a riding habit-style gown, for example, but there is little doubt that the traditional top hat or short, full veil often worn with this particular period style is better suited to the overall silhouette. For this reason it is advisable to try on several types of hats and veils with the gown before making a final decision.

VEILS

A veil made of tulle or net is the traditional form of head-dress worn with a wedding gown. According to author Ann Monserrat, the bridal veil as we know it today is a product of the beginning of the nineteenth century when fashionable women wore a scarf of lace or gauze pinned to the back of the head with the ends wrapped around their bare arms. As a result, says Monserrat, many fashion journals continued to refer to bridal veils as "scarves" in the early decades of the nineteenth century. This fashion has endured as a lasting tradition for brides, although it was briefly eclipsed by a trend for hats during this century.

According to one of the many superstitions surrounding bridalwear, an old veil is supposed to bring good luck to the bride and a borrowed veil even more so. If a bride intends wearing a veil that is a family heirloom, it is wise to take it to the bridal boutique or dressmaker on the first visit and ask their advice on the style of dress best suited to it. Colour, too, is an important consideration in this instance because antique lace or silk tulle veils can discolour with age, so a brilliant white satin dress may make an old veil look slightly shabby, whereas a delicate shade of ivory or cream would be the perfect match.

▽ THIS BRIDAL OUTFIT DATING FROM AROUND 1867 FEATURES AN ORNATE VEIL OF BRUSSELS LACE WORN WITH A NARROW CIRCLET OF FLOWERS. THE GOWN ITSELF IS MADE OF SATIN FESTOONED WITH NET AND DECORATED WITH FLORAL POSIES.

There are many different styles of wedding veils available in a variety of tulle, lace and net. The grand, full-length veil (often known as the cathedral-length veil) has a long train that consists of either one layer of tulle or several of varying lengths, creating tiers. With the latter, the top tier is the shortest, worn over the bride's face when she enters the church. This tradition is adopted by many brides, although it is a matter of personal preference. If the veil is to be worn over the face, it is clearly important to choose a style that can be worn in this way with the right headpiece. This type of veil usually covers the whole head and the floral decoration, tiara or cap is placed on top. The veil is then pulled back over the top of the rest of the head-dress at the end of the marriage ceremony.

△ THIS STUNNINGLY SIMPLE BRIDAL
OUTFIT BY COUTURIER YVES SAINT
LAURENT CONSISTS OF A WRAPOVER
BLOUSE AND FULL- LENGTH SILK
BROCADE SKIRT. THE PLAIN VEIL IS
WORN WITHOUT A HEAD-DRESS AND
FEATURES A RUFFLED TRAIN.

Other styles of veil are attached only at the back of the headpiece, leaving the face and top and sides of the hair free.

A bride who wants to wear a grand veil like this but may be wondering what she can do with the mass of tulle at the reception, could consider the rather lovely French tradition of the bride cutting off the lower part of her veil during the reception and giving a piece to each of the guests as a memento of her wedding day. Obviously, a synthetic net veil will need to be chosen for this purpose, which costs a fraction of the price of silk or cotton versions.

While the idea of silk tulle or cotton net for a veil is infinitely more appealing than a synthetic one, it should be noted that different veiling fabrics have different qualities that suit particular styles. Silk tulle, the costliest, is very fragile and tends to hang straight down unless it is heavily starched. In order to create fullness, therefore, many layers of silk tulle are required. It is also easily torn and so heavy beading is unlikely to be possible.

Cotton net is similar in effect to silk tulle, but it has more body and it also tends to crease.

Nylon net, which appeared in the 1950s, is the stiffest type of veiling and so a very full effect can be created in both long and short styles.

Many antique veils are made of lace, which is less transparent than net or tulle but can look stunning with a simple gown.

Although net, tulle and lace are the most commonly used fabrics for veils, any sheer or transparent fabric, say chiffon, voile or even crisp organza, can be used for a more unusual veil. Indeed, a length of silk chiffon is perfect for the floating chemise-dresses of the 1920s described later.

Veils can be as simple or decorative as personal taste (and finances) dictate. They can be beaded with seed pearls and glass beads, embroidered all over or feature embroidered, scalloped edges. Veil edges can also be trimmed with lace or bound in silk fabric to match the gown. Whatever the style, however, the veil must be securely held in place and the heavier it is, the more securely it needs to be attached.

FLOWERS, JULIET CAPS, TIARAS...

There are numerous ways of fixing the veil – the most popular being a floral headpiece made from silk or fresh flowers. These can be anything from a deep circlet of fresh flowers to the simplest silk rose attached to a haircomb.

The Juliet cap, a small skull cap, is another popular head-dress that fits snugly over the veil. It can be made in the same fabric as the gown and decorated with embroidery or beading.

A family heirloom tiara can also be worn with the bridal veil by those fortunate enough to own one, although less expensive imitation ones can also look very effective.

The style of the dress, veil and bouquet should all be taken into consideration when choosing a head-dress, as should the shape of the bride's face and the hairstyle that will be worn on the day.

HATS

Not everybody wants clouds of tulle and for these brides hats provide plenty of alternatives. A hat can form the focal point of a bridal ensemble and has the practical attraction of being able to be worn again after the wedding.

There are many talented hatters around whose millinery masterpieces defy all notions of a hat being simply a brim and a crown. Fashion magazines and the editorial fashion pages of national newspapers are a good source of information regarding both established and up-and-coming milliners. Alternatively, a plain hat can be decorated to match a wedding gown, with clusters of fresh or silk flowers or, perhaps, swathes of tulle wrapped around the hat which gives a modern illusion of the traditional veil.

▽ RICCIO'S ROMANTIC OFF-THE-SHOULDER WEDDING GOWN HAS A FITTED BODICE AND TULLE SLEEVES THAT HAVE BEEN RICHLY DECORATED WITH LACE AND BEADING. THE ENORMOUS SKIRT IS FASHIONED FROM LAYERS OF SILK TULLE OVER SILK UNDERSKIRTS.
© *Lazaro for Riccio, New York*

▷ SATIN HEADBANDS AND CIRCLETS ARE DECORATED WITH TINY SEED PEARLS AND RHINESTONES BY DESIGNER FLORENCIO MOGADO. THE MATCHING EARRINGS ARE MADE USING PEARLS, RHINESTONES AND TINY COLOURED GLASS BEADS.

▷ MOST BRIDES OPT FOR EXTRAVAGANT WEDDING SHOES FAR REMOVED FROM EVERYDAY FOOTWEAR. LUXURIOUS FABRICS, EMBROIDERY AND BEADING ARE FEATURES OF MANY BRIDAL SHOES. HANNAH GOLDMAN'S CUBAN-HEEL SHOES ARE DECORATED WITH PEARL-EDGED BOWS AND ROSETTES.

▷ FLORENCIO MOGADO'S CLOCHE-SHAPED BRIDAL HATS, INSPIRED BY THE 1920S, ARE EXQUISITELY EMBELLISHED WITH BEADS AND PEARLS. THE HAT ON THE RIGHT HAS MOTHER-OF-PEARL BUTTONS SEWN ONTO IT AND IS EDGED WITH PEARLS AND TINY COLOURED GLASS BEADS.

△ LORENZO RIVA'S LEAF- PATTERNED DAMASK GOWN HAS A PLAIN ROUND-NECKED BODICE AND LONG, FITTED SLEEVES. THE BRIDAL HEAD-DRESS IS MADE FROM WIRED LEAF SHAPES IN MATCHING FABRIC THAT FITS CLOSELY TO THE HEAD OVER THE NET VEIL.

FINDING INSPIRATION

Inspiration for a wedding gown can come from as wide a range of sources as the imagination allows if the plan is to have a one-off dress designed and made. Films, television, paintings, costume museums and costume history books as well as contemporary fashion and bridal magazines provide endless inspiration for both brides-to-be and designers.

There is little that Hollywood producers like more than a good wedding scene or even the wedding as the main subject of the film plot. Major films and international exhibitions can regularly be seen to be the influence behind fashion designers' collections. The "Juliet dress", for example, which derives its name from the costumes worn in Franco Zeffirelli's 1968 film of *Romeo and Juliet,* with a high waistline and puffed top sleeves in the medieval style, became a popular style for wedding dresses at the time and still is today. Fashion trends take longer to affect mainstream wedding gowns which tend to be more traditional by design. However, it is interesting to note that in January 1993, Helen Fifield of the British *Brides & Setting Up Home* magazine suggested that this might be changing: "Bridalwear has often been considered as something very romantic and not connected to fashion at all but I think that this year some of the shapes and the lines are very close to what you actually see on the catwalk". Although the full-skirted Victorian-style gown is

▽ A WREATH OF SATIN CURLS AND TINY VELVET FLOWERS BY CHAPEAUX CARINE MAKES A SOPHISTICATED BRIDAL HEAD-DRESS AND CAN BE WORN WITH OR WITHOUT A VEIL. THE DRAPED SILK TULLE COLLAR ALSO FEATURES SATIN CURLS AND FLOWERS AT THE FRONT.

still very much in existence, there is a marked trend towards straighter styles, such as the Empire and princess-line gowns as well as the long sheath dress based on eveningwear styles (these styles will be described in greater detail during the course of the book).

Films are a wonderful source of inspiration for wedding gowns as well as giving a good idea of how to accessorize a particular style. One of my own all-time favourite gowns is that worn by the late Audrey Hepburn as Eliza Doolittle in the ballroom scene of the 1963 Hollywood screen version of *My Fair Lady*. Designed by Cecil Beaton, her elegant white gown was cut in the Empire style and encrusted with beads and diamanté. Worn with long, white gloves, a magnificent choker necklace and a tiara head-dress, the gown is actually very similar in line to the new Empire-style gowns that many bridal designers are creating for contemporary brides. Equally inspiring are the enormous picture hats Beaton designed for Hepburn, such as the one she wore for the Ascot scene where she was literally wrapped up like a chocolate box in ribbons and bows.

The influence of more recent films can also be seen in contemporary wedding dress design. The extravagant gowns of eighteenth-century France were perfectly recreated in the costumes for *Dangerous Liaisons*, starring Glenn Close, and are echoed in the bridal gowns featured in Chapter 3, Romantic Brides. Some dresses are literal interpretations of this period style, while others merely incorporate certain design features, such as the pointed bodice decorated with rows of diminishing bows down the front or the close-fitting elbow-length sleeves, featuring tiers of lace frills.

The romance of the English country garden, seen in Merchant Ivory's screen adaptation of E.M. Forster's novel *A Room with a View*, features beautiful examples of Edwardian gowns in pale linens and white embroidered lace. The elegant lines of this period translate perfectly in fine cottons and lace for a summer bride looking for an alternative to the more conventional silks and satins used in wedding gowns. The large decorative hats typical of this period, decked with flowers, feathers and lace, are also a picturesque alternative to the traditional veil and can be worn to stunning effect with either long or short bridal gowns.

▽ Zandra Rhodes' sari-style wedding gown is embroidered with seed pearls and sequins. The sari is tied in the Gujarat style while the choli bodice of pure silk taffeta has matching embroidered sleeves. The pointed hems of the gown are hand rolled and trimmed with pearl droplets.

▷ The extravagant costumes of the film *Dangerous Liaisons* are echoed in this bridal outfit. The ivory satin gown, designed by Catherine Walker, is trimmed with black ribbon and bows, while the wide-brimmed hat by Phillip Somerville is adorned with ostrich feathers and a lace veil.

△ A crown-shaped hat of crushed silk forms the bridal head-dress for Scherrer's bridal outfit. The delicate silk tulle veil sparkles subtly with touches of diamanté.

CULTURAL EXCHANGES

While the Western white wedding is often assumed to be the same in every country there are many customs and traditions particular to individual countries. With emigration and the ever-increasing availability of foreign travel, some customs have been adopted by different countries while others remain unique to their country of origin. Those marrying someone of a different nationality will probably combine the wedding traditions of both countries. However, it is not necessary to have links with a particular culture as an excuse to incorporate their wedding customs.

Many Francophiles opt for the French wedding cake *Croquembouche*, which is a pyramid of choux pastry balls covered in a caramelized sugar paste instead of the traditional tiered fruit cake iced in white. The *Croquembouche*, although of French origin, is also the usual wedding cake in other parts of Europe. The cake can be left undecorated or adorned with sugared almonds and lengths of ribbon to match the bridal gown.

The Italian tradition of giving *confetti* to the wedding guests is a custom that has been adopted by many non-Italian brides. Although "confetti" is the word usually used in English to mean the paper symbols thrown at the bride and groom, in Italy it refers to the small parcels of sweets that are distributed at both weddings and christenings as a memento of the occasion. There is a wonderful scene in the film *Godfather II* at a Sicilian wedding where the bride and groom walk round the circle of guests in the village square with bowls of *confetti*, which they spoon out to everyone. It is more usual, however, for the sweets to be given in small decorative bags or boxes known as *bonbonnière*. These can simply be made from net and ribbons to match the bride's gown, although a glance at any Italian bridal magazine will show that the tradition has become big business, with companies producing elaborate silk-lined boxes as well as velvet and lace-trimmed bags to hold the *confetti*.

The "rehearsal dinner" is a peculiarly American tradition that has not been adopted elsewhere, but it is an important part of an

▽ A beautiful French CROQUEMBOUCHE. A delightful, unusual and delicious alternative to the traditional tiered fruit cake, the cake is made up of a pyramid of choux pastry balls, covered in caramelized sugar paste.

American wedding and, indeed, can be a grander occasion than the wedding day itself. Despite its misleading name, the rehearsal dinner does not usually involve a rehearsal of the wedding vows, but appears to have been instituted as a way of introducing the family and guests. The rehearsal dinner can be as formal or informal as personal preferences and finances allow – from a garden barbecue to a grand, black tie dinner. Naturally the bride-to-be's choice of gown for this occasion is dictated by the style of the event, but a formal dinner usually requires an evening gown.

British weddings generally tend to be less formal that do American weddings. An afternoon wedding, followed by a garden reception in a marquee is how a traditional British wedding is usually perceived to proceed. It is relatively uncommon in the UK to be married in the early evening, although Jewish weddings are usually held later in the day and followed by a formal dinner. According to *Debrett's Etiquette and Modern Manners* (Book Club Associates, London, 1981), the most popular time of day for a British country wedding is 2.30 p.m. while town weddings are often slightly later – between 3 p.m. and 5 p.m.

The time of day chosen for the marriage ceremony and wedding reception, however, does not usually affect the bride-to-be's choice of gown, which can be as extravagant or plain as she desires. Dress codes for weddings in America are, in general, more complicated than they are in the UK and apply to the bride's choice of outfit too. A recent guide published in the American magazine *Modern Bride* categorized the different types of wedding thus: formal daytime, formal evening, semi-formal daytime, semi-formal evening and informal daytime and evening. According to New York-based dress designer, Helen Morley, the difference between a formal and an informal wedding is usually marked by whether or not the bridal gown features a train. The hour that separates a formal evening wedding and a formal day wedding is 6 p.m. While the bride's *style* of gown for a formal evening wedding remains the same, the choice of *fabric* and *trimmings* is often more elaborate for an evening affair. A long veil is more often worn with a formal wedding gown.

▽ THIS STRAPLESS SATIN GOWN BY ALLISON BLAKE FEATURES A BUSTLED OVERSKIRT AND TRAIN EMBROIDERED WITH OYSTER SHELL MOTIFS THAT ARE REPEATED ON THE MATCHING SATIN "ARMLETS". THE BONED BODICE IS ALSO HEAVILY EMBROIDERED WITH A CHERUB AND SCROLL MOTIF.

◁ Andrea Wilkin's silk dupion gown is inspired by the Juliet dress, with its full puffed sleeves and heavy plaited silk detail around the bodice edges and neckline. The veil is held in place with a matching plaited silk circlet.

▽ Black and white dresses for the bridal attendants provide a dramatic contrast to the bridal gown. Watters & Watters' off-the-shoulder gown is a popular style for older bridesmaids, particularly in America.

2
CLASSIC
BRIDAL STYLES

THERE ARE CERTAIN WEDDING GOWN STYLES, MANY OF THEM BASED ON PERIOD COSTUMES, THAT HAVE BECOME ESTABLISHED AS CLASSIC DESIGNS. THEY INCLUDE THE LOW-WAISTED 1920S DRESS, THE PRINCESS LINE AND THE HIGH-WAISTED EMPIRE STYLE. LIKE MAINSTREAM FASHION, SUCH STYLES ENJOY RECURRING FAVOUR IN THE FASHION CYCLE AND, ALTHOUGH CERTAIN STYLES MAY DECLINE IN POPULARITY FOR SEVERAL YEARS, THEY INVARIABLY RE-APPEAR.

△ THE SIMPLE LINES OF THIS 1960S GOWN WITH A LACE SHOULDER CAPE WOULD NOT BE OUT OF PLACE TODAY, WITH THE CURRENT MOVE TOWARDS SIMPLICITY. BOTH THE GOWN AND THE UNDERSTATED BOUQUET OF LILIES CONTRAST WITH THE ROMANTIC STYLES OF THE 1980S WHERE FULL-BLOWN GOWNS AND ENORMOUS SHOWER BOUQUETS ENJOYED WIDESPREAD POPULARITY.

During the 1980s the influence of Princess Diana's romantic, fairy-tale gown was clearly apparent in bridalwear design. The 1990s appear to herald a move towards simplicity with the princess line, Empire style and slender sheath dresses (which owe more to eveningwear than to romantic wedding gowns) making a comeback. Each time such styles re-appear in bridal fashions, they are contemporary *interpretations* of classic designs and therefore look refreshingly new. Unlike fashion, which can change dramatically from one season to the next, bridalwear design appears to be more static and certain styles can last for several years or longer. According to author Avril Landsell in her book *Wedding Fashions 1860–1980* (Shire Publications) the princess line gown dominated bridal fashions for almost ten years from the 1960s to the 1970s. Many brides-to-be wear their mother's wedding gowns and find that, although they may have been relegated to the "dressing-up box" as antiquated dresses during their childhood, by the time *they* wear them, they have come back into fashion. Ten years ago, a 1960s gown would have looked terribly outdated, but a simple-trained gown in duchesse satin now looks just right.

1920S STYLE

Certain historical styles, such as a 1920s gown based on the flapper dresses of that period, have become timeless classics and a number of bridalwear designers specialize exclusively in producing these gowns. The slender tube dresses and chemise styles of this decade are a point of inspiration for many designers and make an ideal choice, both as full-length and mid calf-length or shorter. The simple lines of this style lend themselves perfectly to the use of intricate laces and embroidered fabrics such as Chantilly and guipure laces, hand-embroidered tulle and beaded chiffons. On a more practical note, the narrow silhouette of the chemise dress requires less fabric than a full-skirted gown and so costlier fabrics can be used economically. Fabrics for tunic- and chemise-style dresses need to be fluid and drape well for best effect, and such fabrics include georgette, silk satin, washed silk and crêpe de Chine. There are also perfectly acceptable synthetic versions of these fabrics as well as good-quality rayons that all have excellent draping qualities.

Design details of this period style include layered overskirts, apron-style tunics and tabards, which were often originally made in a sheer, contrasting fabric. Petal-edged and scalloped hems, as well asymmetric handkerchief points and drapery, also feature on skirts. The overskirt, which features frequently on 1920s-style gowns, can dip to form a train at the back. Alternatively, a detachable train can hang either from the shoulders or the hip and can be removed after the church ceremony if required.

A "chemise" top to this style of gown derives its name from the French term for a linen undergarment and is a sleeveless shape with a loose cut rather like a vest, while the "camisole" usually features narrow straps over the shoulders. Rows of beads, such as seed pearls, diamanté or even silk flowers, can be used to decorate the straps of a camisole top.

The tube or chemise dress can be straight up and down or feature the dropped waistline with hip sash that is most typically associated with gowns of this period.

△ TWENTIETH CENTURY FROCKS' ANTIQUE LACE GOWN HAS A FRILLED UNDERSLIP OF SILK SATIN. THE 1920S GOWN IS ACCESSORIZED WITH THE BAR SHOES AND CLOCHE HAT TYPICAL OF THAT PERIOD.

▷ This contemporary interpretation of the ever-popular 1920s-style gown by Lyn Lundie, is made in ivory tulle and hand-embroidered with flowers and ferns. The matching fan is decorated with ferns and flowers and is an original replacement for the traditional floral bouquet.

▽ Catherine Buckley's 1920s-style bridal gown and flower-girl's dress are worn with delicate wired and beaded head-dresses. The bridal headband is worn low on the forehead and the delicate lace veil is draped from the back of the band and falls softly over the shoulders.

36

△ A SELECTION OF BRIDAL GLOVES BY
CAROLINA AMATO INCLUDE SHEER LACE,
APPLIQUÉD LACE INSETS BEADED WITH
PEARLS, SILK FLORAL DECORATIONS AND
SEED PEARLS.

◁ AFFINITI'S ANKLE-LENGTH LACE AND
PRINCESS CHIFFON GOWN IS DESIGNED IN
THE 1920S STYLE. THE TEA-LENGTH SKIRT
OF THIS PERIOD STYLE ALSO MAKES IT A
POPULAR CHOICE FOR TROPICAL ISLAND
BRIDES.

As most 1920s-style gowns are knee- or calf-length, the bride's choice of shoes and hosiery is an important element in the overall effect. The shoes typical of the period, often called bar shoes, combine a low cuban heel with a T-bar or single strap over the instep. Decorative fastenings such as small, covered buttons or diamanté buckles appear on such shoes, with soft suede, satin or brocade being favoured materials for the body of the shoes. This shoe style is similar to that worn for contemporary tapdancing and can usually be found at suppliers of dancewear shoes at very reasonable prices. The added advantage of wearing dance footwear as wedding shoes is that they are invariably comfortable as they are made for dancers. If the gown and the attendants' outfits are being made, 0.5 m (nearly ⅔ yd) of extra fabric will be needed to cover the shoes to match the dress.

▽ BAR SHOES COMPLEMENT PERFECTLY THE SLIGHTLY SHORTER-LENGTH 1920S-STYLE DRESSES.

A classic head-dress for a 1920s-style gown is a circular band worn low on the forehead with the veil also fitted closely over the head. The band can be decorated with fresh flowers and most florists can create this type of head-dress using a wire base. Other types of band are made of wire and decorated with beads or metal leaves rather like a tiara.

All-lace veils or lace-edged tulle draped from the headband and falling delicately over the shoulders echo the fluid lines of this style of gown. If a hat is to be worn instead of a traditional veil, a cloche hat in a soft fabric such as velvet, worn pulled down low over the forehead gives an authentic touch.

A small spray of fresh blooms or silk flowers makes a pretty decoration on the sash of a low-waisted gown. Photographs of weddings in the 1920s depict brides with a variety of different bouquets. Many of them were enormous affairs, with long trails of ivy that literally covered the front of the bride's gown, while others consisted of a simple sheaf of white lilies, carried in the crook of the arm. The less formal bunch or sheaf of flowers tied with double-faced satin ribbon is a popular style of bouquet to carry with this style of gown.

EDWARDIAN STYLE

The elegant lines of Edwardian costumes marked a transition from the full-skirted crinolines and bustles of the Victorian era towards a more slender-skirted silhouette. Gowns of this period are often lavishly decorated with lace, braiding, embroidery, pintucking and appliqué. Bridal dresses inspired by the lace tea party gowns of the Edwardian era have proved to be a successful alternative to the full-skirted romantic wedding style.

Typical features of the Edwardian style are the panelled skirt shaped over the hips and flaring to the ankles with emphasis on the back where wider panels form a train. Edwardian daywear featured high necklines on blouses and dresses while evening gowns had low-cut *décolletée*. Wedding gowns of this period, however, usually featured the high neckline that appeared in daywear designs, although it was usually fashioned from a sheer fabric, such as lace. The use of rich braids and applied trimmings as well as heavy lace fabrics are also typical of this period. Softer fabrics also began to replace the stiff taffetas of the Victorian era.

The Edwardian-style gown emphasizes the waistline, while the shapely skirt with a train adds length to the overall silhouette. For those who prefer not to bare all, the high neckline so typical of blouses and dresses of this period can be made in sheer lace and worn over a plain bodice.

A typical feature of the Edwardian blouse is the shoulder-cape effect, often achieved by using a square-shaped piece of lace with a neckline cut in the centre. This is a good way of covering the shoulders otherwise revealed by a strapless or low-cut dress during the marriage ceremony. It could also feature a high neck made of lace and fastened down the back with buttons so that it can be taken off later for the wedding reception or party.

Large picture hats adorned with flowers, feathers, bows and lace (often featuring a face veil) are typical of Edwardian daytime fashions and they balanced the decorative trains that appeared on the skirts. A ready-made hat can be decorated with silk flowers and lace to match the bridal gown for a less formal wedding.

▷ LYN LUNDIE'S EDWARDIAN-STYLE
TEA GOWN IN FRAGILE WHITE LACE
FEATURES A GENTLE TRAIN, SILK BOW
SASH TIED AT THE BACK OF THE SKIRT.
THE BRIDE'S HAIR IS WORN UP TO
EMPHASIZE THE BODICE DETAILS.

△ THE EDWARDIAN-STYLE MOTORING
OUTFIT IS THE INFLUENCE BEHIND
DESIGNER ANDREA WILKIN'S SILK BRIDAL
GOWN. THE FRONT OF THE SKIRT IS SLIM
WHILE THE BACK FLARES OUT TO A
FISHTAIL TRAIN.

EMPIRE STYLE

The simple Empire line, with its high waist positioned just below the bust, has enjoyed recurring popularity in the fashion cycle during the twentieth century – from the late 1900s with the Parisian couturier Paul Poiret, through to the 1960s when the childlike fashions epitomized in photographs of the model Twiggy embraced this style. Worn, too, by Audrey Hepburn in the Hollywood screen version of *My Fair Lady*, an Empire-style gown is a simple and elegant alternative to the full-skirted Victorian silhouette.

The style was adopted by French women during the French Revolution in the late eighteenth century and provided a dramatic contrast to the sartorial excesses of the preceding decades. Named after the French Empress Josephine, the Empire line dress features a high waistline, cut just below the bust, from which the skirt falls straight to the ground. The back of the skirt, which often incorporates a train, is usually set over a small "bustle pad" that holds the fabric clear of the curves of the back of the body so it falls smoothly to the ground. This is a useful dress-making tip and a bustle pad can easily be sewn into a contemporary Empire line gown.

The Empire line gown is particularly flattering to the petite figure because the skirt, falling from the bust rather than the natural waistline, makes the wearer look taller. This expanse of fabric falling from the bustline also creates the perfect foil for embroidery, beading or applied decoration such as silk flowers.

The most popular of the fabrics used for eighteenth-century gowns were fine cotton lawn and muslin, which were often heavily embroidered in self-coloured threads. The

▽ GOLD LACE AND ROWS OF PEARLS ARE USED TO DECORATE ANGEL AND BERMANS' EMPIRE-STYLE GOWN, WHICH FEATURES PUFFED SLEEVES AND A LONG TRAIN OVER A STRAIGHT UNDERDRESS.

flowing qualities of these fabrics can also be achieved using richer fabrics, such as satin-backed crêpe, silk satin and washed silk, which has a wonderful velvety feel. A plain underskirt may be overlaid with a transparent, embroidered fabric that can be used on its own for fragile-looking sleeves. The bodice of an Empire gown is often fashioned from a decorative fabric, such as heavy guipure lace or ribbon lace over plain silk or satin, while sashes or bows fastened below the bustline are another popular feature on this type of gown.

Because of its high waistline, the choice of jacket for a winter wedding is somewhat restricted. The spencer, which is a short jacket without tails, is the perfect solution as its high waistline fits neatly over an Empire gown. A spencer jacket could be made in matching fabric or contrasting plain or patterned fabric, such as velvet or brocade.

The elegant silhouette of the Empire line style works well with grand, full-length veils, particularly when the veil is worn piled up on the head to give added height. A shorter lace veil fixed to the hair with a matching lace bow is a simple gesture that is easy to wear and can be removed easily for the reception without disturbing the hairstyle too much. For a more authentic eighteenth-century style, however, long white feathers could be incorporated into the head-dress.

There are several styles of footwear that complement the Empire gown – the most authentic being flat, ballet-style satin or suede slippers in white or ivory. However, satin-covered mules or low-heeled court shoes are also good alternatives.

Elbow-length gloves look particularly elegant with the Empire style. Gloves can, however, pose a difficulty during the exchanging of the rings but this is a minor problem.

The simplicity of the Empire line gown leaves plenty of scope regarding the choice of flowers and style of the bridal bouquet. In keeping with the slender lines of the gown, a sheaf of long-stemmed lilies tied with a satin ribbon echo the bride's silhouette, while a more ornate arrangement of cascading flowers and trailing leaves can form a stunning focal point.

▽ THE CROPPED SPENCER JACKET HERE COMPLEMENTS THE HIGH-WAISTED EMPIRE STYLE. THE FIGURED SILK JACKET FROM ANGEL AND BERMANS FEATURES A CONTRASTING SHAWL COLLAR AND MINIATURE TAILS.

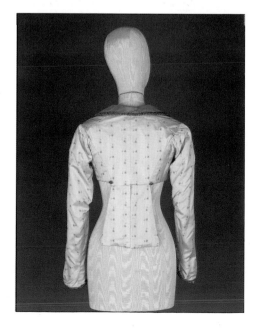

▷ Laura Ashley's lace "jabot" veil is a style that works well with the simple silhouette of an Empire-style gown. It is fastened to the hair with a lace bow and foliage decoration.

△ Slip-on mules in pastel-coloured silks and satins complement an Empire-style gown. These two styles by Gina are in duchesse satin. The ivory satin version features a shaped vamp and flat soles, while the pale pink ones feature a medium-height heel.

◁ Yvonne Damant's contemporary interpretation of the Empire style is fashioned in sheer chiffon over silk. The wide sash wraps over the bustline and is tied at the back, while the shaped hemline features rolled edges.

▽ British designer, John Galliano, frequently looks to the eighteenth century for inspiration for his collections. His Empire-style gown of white muslin is shown damped down so it clings to the figure which, according to some sources, was a method often employed by women during this period.

◁ The Empire-style gown here by Gianfranco Ferre for the house of Dior features a silver and gold embroidered bodice and short, puffed sleeves that are characteristic of the style. The finely pleated skirt hangs straight from beneath the bustline and features gold and silver embroidery around the hem.

THE PRINCESS LINE

Along with the Empire style, the princess line is one of the newest silhouettes in bridal gowns, reflecting the general trend towards simplicity that appears to be shaping bridalwear for the future. After all the lace, ruffles and enormously full skirts of the 1980s, this move towards simplicity is perhaps a logical one. The princess line was chosen by Lady Helen Windsor for her marriage in 1991. The dress was designed by French couturier Catherine Walker, whose couture house The Chelsea Design Company is also a favourite haunt of the Princess of Wales.

The princess line features a close-fitting bodice, cut so that there is no waist seam, that flares out in panels to form a full skirt. The style is said to have been invented by the couturier Charles Worth in the 1860s for a dress he designed for the Empress Eugenie. This flattering shape has been used for both bridal gowns and coatdresses and was extremely popular during the 1960s and 1970s. It is interesting to note that the new simplicity emerging in the design of wedding gowns harks back to the 1960s and 1970s. Many of the gowns of the 1960s and 1970s were also Empire style and, according to Avril Landsell in her book *Wedding Fashions 1860–1980*, these styles dominated bridal fashions for almost ten years. The simplistic style of Princess Anne's wedding gown is closer to many contemporary bridal fashions than the more romantic mood of Princess Diana's gown. Ideal fabrics for princess line gowns are duchesse satin, silk brocades and fine corded silk. Fabrics for this style need to have a certain amount of body in order to hold the flared shape well. Beading or decoration when applied to a princess line gown is usually worked on the bodice area of the dress, while the flared panels of the skirt are left unadorned. Even so, emphasis is placed on fabric and cut rather than trimmings.

The pronounced shape of the princess line skirt with its flared panels can be set off very effectively by a shorter veil. A short, full style, comprising several layers of net or tulle falling to just below the shoulders or to above the waistline, echoes the silhouette of the princess line.

△ JULIET POYSER'S PRINCESS LINE BRIDAL COAT IN DUCHESSE SATIN FEATURES A HIGH STANDAWAY COLLAR AND COVERED BUTTONS. THE CLOSE-FITTING BODICE FLARES OUT IN PANELS TO FORM THE WIDE SKIRT, WHICH IS SUPPORTED BY LAYERS OF NET BENEATH.

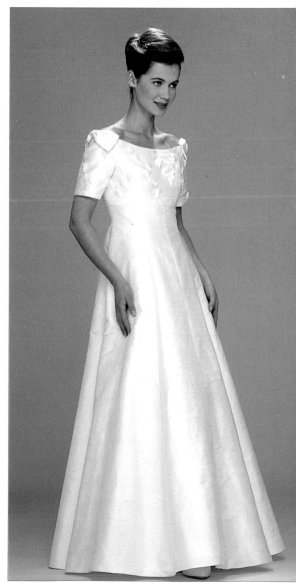

▽ ALLISON BLAKE'S SHORT-SLEEVED
PRINCESS LINE GOWN IN DUPION SILK HAS
A BOAT-SHAPED NECKLINE DECORATED
WITH PLAIN SILK BOWS, WHILE THE
BODICE FEATURES CLUSTERS OF TINY SEED
PEARLS. THIS STYLE IS TYPICAL OF THE
CLEAN, UNCLUTTERED SILHOUETTE
USUALLY ASSOCIATED WITH A PRINCESS
LINE GOWN.

△ CATHERINE DAVIGHI'S PRINCESS
LINE BRIDAL COAT IS CUT IN THE
DOUBLE-BREASTED STYLE WITH A *FICHU*
COLLAR. THE SCROLL MOTIF ON THE
COLLAR AND THE BUTTONS ARE WORKED
IN ROWS OF TINY SEED PEARLS.

▽ CATHERINE RAYNER'S WHITE SATIN SHEATH DRESS IS HEAVILY ENCRUSTED WITH PEARLS AND RHINESTONES AROUND THE SCOOPED NECKLINE. THE GOWN ALSO FEATURES MATCHING "ARMLETS" AND A CHOKER NECKLACE, BOTH OF WHICH ARE BEADED WITH PEARLS.

THE SHEATH DRESS

The slender sheath dress, often featuring a detachable train, is a particularly elegant style for an evening wedding. A detachable train makes for a dramatic entrance to the church, but can be removed for the wedding reception, creating a totally different look. Bodices can be strapless, off-the-shoulder or with sleeves, while ankle-length skirts often feature fishtail trains which make them easier to walk in. On the other hand, a straight sheath dress will usually feature a slit or deep pleat at the back for this purpose.

Fabrics for straight or sheath dresses should be chosen carefully as they can crease badly across the lap area after sitting down. A good-quality lining fabric should prevent creases occurring to some degree, but a very fine silk fabric will tend to wrinkle nonetheless. Heavier weight fabrics, such as duchesse satin, crêpe or corded silk, will hang better and are less prone to creasing. Furthermore, a long train will tend to drag somewhat where it is attached at the back of the dress if the dress fabric is very fine.

The fishtail gown has a slender silhouette that flares out from the knee or below in panels or *godets*. While retaining a slim-fitting overall silhouette, the fullness near the hem makes it easier to walk in than a sheath dress.

Many fishtail gowns are cut on the bias and are reminiscent of the slinky satin dresses worn by Hollywood movie stars of the 1930s. The bias cut is said to have been invented by the French couturier Madeleine Vionnet in the 1920s, although this style of gown is perhaps better associated with the 1930s evening gowns, many of which were created by the costume designer Adrian in Hollywood and worn by actresses such as Jean Harlow.

The wide variety of sheath and fishtail-style gowns can easily be accessorized with veils, head-dresses and shoes. The veil should echo the length and style of the train, if the gown has one, while shoes of a medium heel height are preferable to flat shoes. Shoes are usually quite visible beneath a straight gown and so an elegant shape in a beautiful fabric tends to look more stylish than a fussy over-decorated style.

▽ THIS SLENDER SHEATH DRESS BY LORENZO RIVA FEATURES A FULL TULLE TRAIN ATTACHED TO THE BACK OF THE SKIRT. THE SKIRT FABRIC IS OF HEAVY CROCHET-STYLE LACE, WHICH IS ECHOED IN THE POLKA DOT MOTIFS ON THE TRAIN.

▷ EAST MEETS WEST IN YUMI KATSURA'S WEDDING GOWN OF BRILLIANT WHITE SATIN, WHICH FEATURES A SLENDER SHEATH AND A MATCHING KIMONO-STYLE COAT WITH A DEEP TRAIN. BOTH ARE RICHLY EMBROIDERED AND BEADED WITH SEED PEARLS.

△ THIS SILK DUPION SHEATH GOWN BY
BRIDES INTERNATIONAL IS DECORATED
WITH LAVENDER-BLUE SILK ROSES. THE
GOWN AND DETACHABLE TRAIN ARE
BOTH TRIMMED IN AUSTRIAN GUIPURE
EMBROIDERY. WITHOUT THE TRAIN, THE
WEDDING GOWN CAN BE WORN FOR A
FORMAL EVENING RECEPTION.

◁ PHILLIPPA LEPLEY'S SLENDER FULL-
LENGTH GOWN IN IVORY AND OYSTER-
COLOURED DUCHESSE SATIN, FEATURES A
GRAND BUSTLE TIED IN A HUGE BOW AT
THE BACK, DECORATED WITH OSTRICH
PLUMES. THE MODEL WEARS SATIN
"ARMLETS". THESE ARE A PRACTICAL
ALTERNATIVE TO LONG GLOVES, WHICH
USUALLY HAVE TO BE REMOVED DURING
THE EXCHANGING OF THE MARRIAGE
BANDS.

3
ROMANTIC
BRIDES

THE MOST ENDURINGLY POPULAR STYLE FOR WEDDING

DRESSES IS THE FULL-BLOWN ROMANTIC GOWN WITH FITTED

BODICE AND FULL SKIRT, GATHERED AT THE TOP, OFTEN

FEATURING A TRAIN AT THE BACK. FAR-REMOVED FROM

ORDINARY, EVERYDAY DRESS, THIS ENCHANTING STYLE

RECALLS ANOTHER ERA AND IS PART OF THE FAIRY-TALE

PORTRAYAL OF WEDDINGS THAT WE SEE IN FILMS AND READ IN

LITERATURE THROUGHOUT OUR LIVES.

▽ THE INFLUENCE OF THE PRINCESS OF WALES' WEDDING GOWN IS SEEN IN KENZO'S BRIDAL OUTFIT FOR SPRING/ SUMMER 1982 – THE GROOM WAS EVEN DRESSED AS PRINCE CHARLES IN NAVAL UNIFORM.

Martha Stewart notes in her book *Weddings* (Sidgwick & Jackson, London, 1987) that, according to Alfred Angelo (who is one of America's largest bridalwear manufacturers), the gowns that sell least well are the up-to-date fashions. British shoe designer Emma Hope agrees that "When people get married they often change completely and they wear things that they'd never wear otherwise. People want things that are quite historical – with a feeling of bygone times".

There are many theories about why it is so popular to adopt what is really a form of fancy dress for the wedding day. Writer Alison Lurie has suggested that perhaps "the function of the white wedding dress and veil is magical; that by putting it on the bride cancels out her previous experiences, so that she may enter marriage emotionally and symbolically".

Whatever the reasons for its longstanding favour, it is the romantic style of gown that is perhaps most often associated with Western weddings. Bridalwear designer Juliet Poyser, whose signature designs are simple, unfussy gowns, says that in Japan many brides-to-be have chosen one of her creations for a Western-style wedding only to have their mothers insist upon the more traditional full-blown gowns that they associate with the West.

It was the romantic style Lady Diana Spencer chose for her wedding gown when she married Prince Charles in July 1981 and it led to a huge revival of this style. The first copy of the dress reputedly arrived in Debenhams' shop window just five hours after the marriage ceremony took place. The original was designed by David and Elizabeth Emanuel and was an ivory silk taffeta gown, featuring a boned bodice with puffed sleeves that were trimmed with silk flounces and layers of lace that had been specially dyed to match the fabric of the gown. The skirt extended at the back to form a train and the dress also had a detachable court train measuring 7.6 m (25 ft) in length that was worn for the service at St Paul's. The ivory-coloured bobbinet lace veil worn by Lady Diana was embellished with pearl sequins and worn with a diamond tiara that belonged to her family. The brides's shoes were made of matching silk, sewn with sequins and fabric rosettes, while the soles were painted with flowers. Described at the time by many as the "wedding of the century", the publicity that surrounded the wedding gown clearly influenced bridalwear designers in the following years, just as the new Princess's interest in fashion since then has affected most areas of the fashion industry. Even the design of Lady Diana's engagement ring was immediately copied by the British high street jeweller Ratners and 40,000 of them were sold in the first year alone and they continued to sell well for several years afterwards.

▽ AN OFF-THE-SHOULDER BODICE WITH SHORT, FITTED SLEEVES IS CREATED IN HEAVY BEADED LACE SEWN WITH PEARLS, WHILE THE FULL SKIRT OF TULLE IS DECORATED WITH LACE MOTIFS. THE BRIDE WEARS A SIMPLE THREE- STRAND PEARL CHOKER AND LONG WHITE GLOVES.

△ HUNDREDS OF LAYERS OF SILK TULLE
ARE USED HERE TO CREATE THE FULL
SKIRT OF VICTOR EDELSTEIN'S GOWN.
THE STRAPLESS BODICE HAS A SHEER
TOP, COVERING THE NECK AND
SHOULDERS, THAT IS EMBROIDERED WITH
SILK APPLIQUÉ MOTIFS.

▷ SILK FLOWERS AND LEAVES FORM THE
FOCAL POINT OF THIS ROMANTIC DRESS
BY STEVIE'S GOWNS. THE COLOURED
BLOOMS ADORN THE OFF-THE-SHOULDER
NECKLINE AND PUFFED SLEEVES AND
FOLLOW THE LINE OF THE SHAPED BODICE
AT THE BACK OF THE DRESS.

◁ FULL, PUFFED SLEEVES IN PALE PEACH
TAFFETA FORM ENORMOUS ROSETTES ON
BEN YEUNG'S BRIDAL GOWN. THE FULL
SKIRT IS ST'FFENED WITH LAYERS OF NET
BOUND IN MATCHING SILK RIBBON.

▷ A RE-EMBROIDERED LACE BODICE
ENCRUSTED WITH BEADS FEATURES ON
THIS WEDDING GOWN DESIGNED BY MISS
JENNY OF ITALY. THE SILK SKIRT IS
FASHIONED FROM LAYERS OF PETALS
GATHERED ONTO THE DROPPED
WAISTLINE OF THE BODICE OF THE DRESS,
WHILE THE BRIDAL HEAD-DRESS IS
CREATED WITH LAYERS OF RUCHED NET.

▽ The Duchess of York's ivory satin gown, designed by Lindka Cierach, featured a traditional court train, embroidered with the initials of the bride and groom.

Design features

The romantic full-skirted wedding gown with a long train ensures a dramatic entrance and part of its appeal is undoubtedly its fairy-tale associations, being far removed from the kinds of outfits worn every day. There are numerous variations on the full-skirted gown with fitted bodice, ranging from the plainest silk creation without adornment to diamanté-encrusted satins, featuring embroidered cutwork in silver threads. Other designs introduce colour in details such as silk, hand-painted or embroidered flowers, scrolls and contrast piping along the seams.

The design of a romantic wedding gown can be altered to flatter all kinds of figures. For example, a short waist can be visually elongated by having a slightly lowered waistline or stomacher-style bodice (a decorative section of material often seen on historical gowns). A slightly raised waistline, which creates a shorter bodice, gives an illusion of added length to the lower half of the body. A V or triangular shape on the bodice flatters the figure, making the waist appear smaller. Different fabrics can also be combined in one style. Popular options include heavy lace or beaded bodices with plain silk or full net skirts.

The full skirts on romantic-style gowns, which can use a great deal of fabric depending on the degree of fullness required, can be pleated or gathered on to the bodice. For a more streamlined dress, the skirt will be cut in panelled sections that skim over the hips and flare out at the hem. Like gathered skirt styles, the panels can be cut as wide as required and a popular feature is to cut them more generously at the back to create a sweeping train. This particular method was employed by British-based designer Lindka Cierach for the gown worn by Sarah Ferguson at her marriage to Prince Andrew in 1986. In addition to the full skirt train, Sarah Ferguson wore a court train, attached at the waist.

It is interesting to note that wedding dresses of the past invariably featured high necklines and long sleeves and many brides follow this convention of covering the neck and arms if the marriage ceremony is to take place in a church or synagogue.

Contemporary interpretations of period gowns featuring low-cut or off-the-shoulder necklines are more likely to be based on evening gowns or court dress of that period. According to Joanna Marschner, Assistant Curator of the Court Dress Collection at Kensington Palace in London, a wedding dress was often worn for presentation at Court and would have to be altered in accordance with the rules that dictated a low neckline, short sleeves and a long court train. For this reason, wedding gowns often featured detachable sleeves and bodices were folded down to reveal "the appropriate line of *décolletage*". Such design details are still incorporated in wedding gowns today so that the bride may change the gown so that it is more revealing.

As with all wedding gowns it is important to give as much consideration to the back view of the dress as to the front. While the front of the gown will be visible in the wedding photographs, the back view is what will be seen during the marriage ceremony. A sweeping train, which can be part of the skirt itself or a separate length of fabric, is one way of ensuring a dramatic entrance for the bride. However, it is important to bear in mind certain practical factors, such as the size of the church – a sweeping train looks fine in a large cathedral or church, but it is likely to just get in the way in a small chapel. A trained skirt can also be a problem at a reception, where it may get trampled underfoot. Most designers ensure that the trains can be looped up to form a bustle. This is usually done by means of hidden ribbons or ties that draw the train up and off the floor. Other trains feature a loop or ribbon that can simply be held by the bride while she is walking around so that the train can be easily let down again for the wedding photographs.

Skirts and trains on romantic gowns can be as decorative or as plain as desired, echoing details of the bodice or simply a dramatic sweep of lustrous satin or silk. Decoration on a train depends on the type and weight of fabric employed in the gown itself. Satin, whether heavy duchesse made from real silk or one of the less costly synthetic varieties, lends itself perfectly to heavy beading and embroidery as well as cutwork, while fragile silk or paper taffeta is unsuitable for this kind of decoration. This was a problem

▽ RAPSIMO'S IVORY SATIN GOWN FEATURES A HEAVY LACE BODICE AND FULL-LENGTH SLEEVES BEADED WITH SEED PEARLS. THE SATIN TRAIN AND MATCHING TULLE VEIL ARE EMBROIDERED WITH LACE MOTIFS, HIGHLIGHTED WITH PEARLS.

encountered by Lindka Cierach, who found that English satin was unsuitable as ground fabric for heavy beading, which was an important feature of Sarah Ferguson's gown. Joanna Marschner, co-author of the book *The Royal Wedding Dresses* points out that the ivory silk duchesse satin had to be imported from Italy.

Beadwork is an attractive, though expensive, feature on wedding gowns and looks particularly dramatic on trains. Seed pearls, which have long been a traditional feature on wedding gowns, bugle beads (tiny glass tube-shaped beads), irridescent mother-of-pearl sequins and diamanté beads add depth and sparkle to fabric. Beaded designs may incorporate flowers, religious symbols or even a family crest. A particularly attractive feature of Sarah Ferguson's train was the intertwined initials A and S sewn in silver beads. Such methods can be done by a designer or dressmaker.

Another way of decorating a skirt or train is with flowers, which can be either fresh blooms or fashioned from matching or coloured silks. The use of fresh flowers, notably orange blossom, was very fashionable in Victorian times when gowns were literally covered with drapes of flowers and greenery such as ivy trails. Writer Avril Landsell notes in her book, *Wedding Fashions 1860–1980*, that, "The comment was made of many Victorian royal brides that they were 'sunk in greenery and resembled walking flower gardens' and that 'Those who could afford to made their weddings as much like the royal ones as possible'". Today, fresh flower decorations are more often than not kept solely for the bride's head-dress and bouquet, fabric rosettes or artificial silk flowers being used to adorn the gown itself. Flowers and rosettes are a good way of introducing an element of colour into a white or ivory gown and can echo the theme of the attendants' outfits as well as the wedding flowers. Red or green are popular colours for winter weddings, both of which look dramatic against a brilliant white gown. A wreath of red silk roses around a low neckline makes an unusual alternative to lace or ruffles, while clusters of peach roses on a background of appliquéd and silk leaves following the line of a bodice and train of an otherwise simple white gown are very attractive. The same floral decorations can also be part of the bride's bouquet and head-dress.

△ SNOW WHITE SATIN IS EMBELLISHED WITH DIAMANTÉ AND SILVER THREAD CUTWORK ON THIS GOWN BY ALFRED ANGELO. THE DESIGN INCORPORATES A SWEETHEART NECKLINE AND SHORT SLEEVES WHILE THE DRAMATIC, LONG TRAIN IS WORKED WITH EMBROIDERY AND BEADING TO MATCH THE GOWN.

▷ A FITTED BODICE FASTENED WITH TINY COVERED BUTTONS FEATURES FULL PUFFED SLEEVES, QUILTED WITH TINY SILK ROSES. THE SKIRT IS GATHERED AT THE BACK OF THE WAIST TO FORM FOLDS LIKE PETALS, WHICH ARE ALSO DECORATED WITH SILK ROSES.

▷ A DROPPED WAISTLINE FEATURES ON THIS WHITE SATIN GOWN BY PRONUPTIA. THE V-SHAPED BODICE IS SEWN WITH SCROLLS OF BRAID AND BEADED WITH SEED PEARLS. THE BRIDAL BOUQUET CONSISTS OF DARK-COLOURED FLOWERS, WHICH MAKE AN UNUSUAL ALTERNATIVE TO THE TRADITIONAL ALL-WHITE OR IVORY FLOWERS USED IN MANY BOUQUETS.

▷ SIMPLE DETAILS TRANSFORM THIS ALL-WHITE ROMANTIC GOWN BY DESIGNER CATHERINE DAVIGHI. THE FULL, LEG O' MUTTON SLEEVES FEATURE THE TINIEST OF COVERED SILK BUTTONS, WHILE THE BODICE NECKLINE IS DECORATED WITH CLUSTERS OF SILK ROSES IN SOFT PINKS.

THE INFLUENCE OF THE EIGHTEENTH CENTURY

The opulent fashions of eighteenth-century France have been captured in many romantic wedding gowns by bridal designers, where the abundant use of frothy lace, rich brocaded silks, plunging necklines and enormous skirts captured so perfectly in the film *Dangerous Liaisons*, translate perfectly into fairy-tale gowns.

Prominent design features of French gowns of the pre-Revolutionary period are the tightly-fitted bodice, which moulds the bust and compresses the waistline by means of boning or a stomacher, and consists of a decorative triangular section of stiffened fabric inserted at the front of a bodice. Many bodices have *echelles*, which are ribbon bows, diminishing in size, sewn down the centre front. Close-fitting sleeves to the elbow feature layers of lace and ruffles decorated with ribbons and bows. Necklines on bodices were invariably plunging and square-shaped or round in cut. A *fichu*, or scarf, made of fine gauze or lace covered the bare *décolletée* and this particular feature would be ideal for a contemporary bride to wear during the marriage ceremony and it could be removed for the wedding reception.

The myriad styles of gown worn at the French court, described in the many costume history books devoted to this period, provide an endless source of inspiration for both bridalwear designers and the brides-to-be. Many skirts have a draped overskirt, known as the *polonaise*, and an attractive feature of this style is that it can incorporate two types of fabric in the over- and underskirts. For example a brocaded silk overskirt may be combined with a fine silk or lawn underskirt, trimmed with lace and ribbon. For a truly authentic-looking eighteenth-century gown, the perfect choice of fabric is a figured silk, brocade or damask for the bodice, sleeves and overskirt in white, cream or ivory, or even a pale pastel shade such as soft pink or primrose yellow. Underskirts can be created from layers of lace ruffles, muslin or ribbon-trimmed tulle. The stomacher or the whole of the bodice can be a focal point of the gown and can feature embroidery, ribbon bows, beading or lacing.

△ LUSTROUS SATIN IS USED TO MAKE THE BODICE AND OVERSKIRT OF THIS BRIDAL GOWN BY THE WIZARD OF GOS. THE SQUARE-NECKED BODICE IS DECORATED WITH BOWS, WHICH ARE A TYPICAL FEATURE OF EIGHTEENTH-CENTURY GOWNS. THE UNDERSKIRT IS PINTUCKED AND TRIMMED WITH RUFFLED LACE, WHICH IS ALSO USED FOR THE SLEEVE FRILLS.

△ THE OPULENT FASHIONS OF
EIGHTEENTH-CENTURY FRANCE ARE THE
INSPIRATION BEHIND VIVIENNE
WESTWOOD'S GOWN. THE BONED
CORSET-STYLE BODICE HAS FULL SLEEVES
WHILE THE LAYERED SKIRT WITH APRON
IS PRINTED IN GOLD AND SPRINKLED WITH
GLITTER.

△ A CLUSTER OF FLOWERS AND LEAVES
IN PASTEL-COLOURED SILKS IS USED TO
CREATE THIS BRIDAL HEAD-DRESS BY SILK
AND WORN WITH AN EIGHTEENTH
CENTURY-STYLE WEDDING GOWN IN SILK
TAFFETA TRIMMED WITH FINE LACE.

British designer Vivienne Westwood regularly looks to the eighteenth century for inspiration in her collections, which have included the boned corset that has since appeared in the catwalk collections of a number of other international designers. Westwood's extravagant gowns feature her signature boned corset cut with a stomacher-piece that extends to a curved point at the front. Yards of silk tulle sprayed with glitter, form the huge overskirts with white boned crinoline petticoats being worn underneath them, while others come in sugar-pink tulle.

An eighteenth century-style gown provides great scope for accessories, which can be as extravagant as the dress itself. Opaque white hosiery, whether tights or stockings, is the perfect legwear for this style. Slip-on mules or pumps with a Louis heel can echo decorative elements of the gown itself, such as a silk bow or beaded motif. Features of shoes of this period is that the instep of the foot is usually covered with a deep tongue and that they have mid to low heels.

The choice of veil for this type of dress can be anything from a mid- to full-length style to a small lace square held in place with a jewelled comb or fresh flower decoration. A soft, wide-brimmed hat, with or without a veil, and decorated with white feather plumes and flowers is another option for a head-dress.

The fashion for chokers, which were often made from lengths of the actual dress fabric in the eighteenth century, have recently enjoyed a comeback in fashion and these are the perfect accessory for the low *décolleté* necklines of these gowns. The choice of jewellery for a choker is unlimited – from the smallest cameo pinned to a length of ribbon or fabric around the throat to rows of diamanté or faux pearls. For a truly authentic touch, a beauty spot painted on the face could be part of the wedding day make-up.

The choice of bridal bouquet for this romantic style should take into consideration the amount of detail on the skirt of the bridal gown. Panniers, ruching and lace ruffles on a skirt call for a simple bouquet or posy – an ornate array of cascading flowers can look too fussy. A single silk rose or a Victorian-style posy (a plump, rounded shape, often backed with lace) are other floral options.

▽ Eighteenth century- style shoes were often as ornate as the costumes. The contemporary bridal shoe here by designer Peter Fox echoes this period style and features a pleated silk frill and jewelled buckle.

◁ A DRAMATIC HAT CAN BE HIRED FROM A THEATRICAL COSTUMIER, WHICH WILL GUARANTEE AN AUTHENTIC PERIOD FEEL TO THE WEDDING OUTFIT. THE EIGHTEENTH CENTURY-STYLE HAT HERE IS DECORATED WITH LACE, STRIPED SILK RIBBON AND OSTRICH PLUMES.

△ THIS IVORY SILK GOWN DESIGNED BY ANGELA HOLMES FOR DROOPY & BROWNS COMBINES ELEMENTS OF EIGHTEENTH CENTURY STYLE WITHOUT THE EXCESSES. THE FITTED BODICE AND LONG SLEEVES ARE COMPLETELY PLAIN WHILE THE FULL SKIRT IS GATHERED AND RUCHED TO FORM FABRIC ROSETTES.

△ ANTHONY PRICE'S IVORY LACE GOWN FEATURES A FITTED BODICE AND SLEEVES WITH LACE FRILL AND BOWS AT THE ELBOW WHILE THE TIERED SILK SKIRT IS EDGED WITH LACE. A LARGE HAT DECORATED WITH OSTRICH PLUMES BY NICHOLAS OAKWELL, AND A VELVET RIBBON CHOKER MAKE APPROPRIATE ACCESSORIES FOR THIS PERIOD STYLE.

▷ THE EXTRAVAGANT HEADGEAR WORN WITH EIGHTEENTH-CENTURY GOWNS IS REFLECTED IN THIS HAT DESIGNED BY PHILIP TREACY FOR FASHION DESIGNER JOHN GALLIANO. THE LIGHTWEIGHT STRUCTURE IS SWATHED IN SILK AND TULLE AND DECORATED WITH OSTRICH PLUMES.

R IDING HABIT STYLES

The riding habit gown is a popular design for both summer and winter brides. While combining the traditional elements of the full-skirted wedding gown, the equestrian style is a dramatic alternative for the bride who feels that lace and ruffles do not suit her. Inspired by the female version of the masculine suit worn for riding and walking in the nineteenth century, the riding habit usually features a tailored jacket fitted at the waist then flaring to either a peplum or tails at the back, worn over a long, full skirt. The two-piece riding habit can also be made as a one-piece dress, featuring a bodice with the traditional leg o' mutton sleeves characteristic of riding costumes. An attractive and practical feature of the riding jacket, however, is that it can conceal a strapless gown to be revealed at the wedding reception or evening party.

Variations on the riding jacket are numerous and feature many different neckline shapes, sleeve and skirt styles without detracting from its distinctive overall effect. These include the tailored collar and rever used on men's jackets, which looks suitably feminine when fashioned in, say, a figured silk or brocade; a round neck with a small Peter Pan collar fastened with rows of tiny, covered buttons. Leg o' mutton (or *gigot*) sleeves, which are generously puffed at the shoulder and taper to fit closely at the wrist are a popular shape for riding jackets, although they can also be plain with deep cuffs and detailed button fastenings. A deep V-shaped neckline with a *fichu* collar, or even an off-the-shoulder shape would appeal to the bride-to-be who likes this style, but feels that the traditional jacket is a little *too* concealing. Jackets can flare into a short peplum from the waistline, or be cutaway at the sides with emphasis at the back. Jacket hems may feature coat tails, pleats or a fluted half-peplum, echoing the skirt train.

A riding habit outfit can combine different colours and fabrics, such as velvet or brocade for the jacket and a billowing paper taffeta for the skirt. Winter weddings offer great scope for introducing rich fabrics and colours to the jacket, such as velvet in

▽ RED IS ALWAYS A POPULAR COLOUR PAIRED WITH WHITE FOR WINTER BRIDES. ANNALIESE SHARP'S SILK RIDING JACKET FEATURES LEG O' MUTTON SLEEVES, TAILS AND IS TRIMMED WITH BLACK ON THE COLLAR AND BUTTONS. THE PLAIN SILK SKIRT SWEEPS OUT DRAMATICALLY AT THE BACK TO FORM A TRAIN.

crimson or hunting green. Fine wool challis or cashmere and wool blends would also lend themselves perfectly to this style. A more tailored jacket shape benefits from the inherent suitability of wool to such techniques, while layers of net underskirts give the requisite fullness to a wool overskirt. A short cape inspired by the traditional highwayman's caped coat makes an ideal warm layer for a winter wedding and can be trimmed with fur around the collar and hem. A fur muff is a practical as well as an attractive accessory for a cold winter's day and a spray of flowers can be attached to the muff as a novel alternative to the conventional bridal bouquet.

Most skirts or dresses made in the equestrian bridal style are fashioned in crisp fabrics, such as taffeta, silk dupion or Thai silk, and worn over petticoats of net or organdie to maintain their fullness. A useful tip when buying petticoats and underskirts for such gowns is to choose ones with a fairly fitted basque top so that the fullness starts at hip level or below, preventing unflattering bunching at the waistline. If the skirt has a full train at the back, the underskirts are often made with more fullness at the back to emphasize this feature.

For those with (or even without) Scottish ancestry, many tartan checks are reproduced on silks that can be used for the riding jacket or as trims on collars, cuffs and covered buttons. Tartan checks are a good way of introducing colour to an all-white or ivory gown and are particularly effective for winter wedding gowns where the fabric can also be used to create the attendants' outfits. On a plain-coloured riding jacket, cornelli work and other embroidery lends itself well to this style, while the dramatic fullness of the skirt looks best left unadorned. Woven braids in rich patterns are also seen on riding jackets and skirts as edgings on collars, cuffs, skirt panels and hems and can be used to make a matching hatband.

Accessories are an important part of achieving the riding habit style. A top hat or similar shape with a deep crown provides the finishing touch for a truly equestrian look. Many bridal milliners make this style in white and ivory as well as stronger colours, although these hats can also be found in most hat shops. A veil in tulle or netting can be attached to the hat and used to cover the

△ THIS VELVET BRIDAL COAT BY BYBLOS FEATURES A MATCHING FUR MUFF TRIMMED WITH A SPRAY OF FLOWERS.

▽ TARTAN CHECK FABRIC IS USED TO CREATE THIS TAILORED BRIDAL JACKET BY UNGARO FOR A WINTER BRIDE. THE BACK OF THE JACKET AND THE EPAULETTES ARE DECORATED WITH FRINGED TASSELS AND PEARL BEADS WHILE THE NECK AND CUFFS ARE MADE OF PLEATED ORGANZA RUFFLES.

▽ A CONTRASTING SILK RIDING JACKET
FEATURES A *FICHU* NECKLINE AND
"TAILS" IN DONNA SALADO'S
EQUESTRIAN BRIDAL OUTFIT WORN
WITH A PLAIN FULL SKIRT. DESIGN
DETAILS ARE PROMINENT ON THE
JACKET, WHICH IS FASTENED WITH TINY,
COVERED BUTTONS THAT ALSO APPEAR
ON THE SLEEVES. THE RIDING HAT IS
DECORATED WITH A MATCHING BAND
AND TRAILING TULLE.

△ THE SUMPTUOUS SATIN RIDING
HABIT STYLES DESIGNED BY KARL
LAGERFELD FOR THE HOUSE OF CHANEL
COMBINE TAILORED JACKETS WITH FULL
SKIRTS FESTOONED WITH SATIN ROSES.
THE SKIRTS ARE INTRICATELY DRAPED
AND SWAGGED AROUND THE HIPLINE
AND FEATURE FULLNESS AT THE BACK.

◁ THE FULL, LEG O' MUTTON SLEEVES
AND LONG, TRAINED SKIRT THAT ARE
TYPICAL FEATURES OF THE RIDING HABIT-
STYLE GOWN ARE INCORPORATED IN THIS
ANTIQUE WHITE SILK GOWN DESIGNED BY
ANGELA HOLMES FOR DROOPY &
BROWNS. THE WHITE SILK TOP HAT
FEATURES A TULLE VEIL WORN OVER THE
FACE.

▷ NICKI HILL'S EMBROIDERED SILK
GOWN IS ACCESSORIZED WITH BRIGHT
ORANGE SILK, WHICH IS USED TO TRIM
THE RIDING HAT. THE BRIDAL BOUQUET
OF ORANGE AND PINK ROSES IS TIED WITH
MATCHING ORANGE SILK RIBBON.

△ VICTORIAN-STYLE RIDING BOOTS
ARE THE PERFECT FOOTWEAR FOR THE
EQUESTRIAN BRIDAL STYLE. THE WHITE
LEATHER BOOTS DESIGNED BY PETER FOX
HAVE A SMALL CURVED HEEL AND LACE-
UP FRONTS. RIDING BOOTS MAY ALSO BE
COVERED IN FABRIC TO MATCH
ATTENDANTS' OUTFITS FOR THIS
PARTICULAR BRIDAL STYLE.

face in the same way as would a traditional veil during the marriage ceremony. A length of tulle tied around the hat can be left trailing down the back to give the illusion of a veil. Otherwise a short veil suits this particular style of gown best for those who prefer a more traditional form of head-dress.

A pair of Victorian-style riding boots with a low heel and side-buttoning or laces are the perfect footwear for the riding habit gown. Many bridal shoe designës include this style in their collections and the boots come in brocade and silks as well as soft leathers and suedes. Short cotton or suede gloves in white or a contrasting colour also make appropriate accessories for the riding habit outfit.

4
MODERN
BRIDES

WHILE THE ROMANTIC, FULL-SKIRTED GOWNS OF THE PAST ARE UNDOUBTEDLY A FAVOURITE SOURCE OF INSPIRATION FOR MANY BRIDES, OTHERS FEEL THAT THIS PARTICULAR STYLE IS JUST NOT SUITED TO THEIR PERSONALITY OR TASTE. FURTHERMORE, A LENGTHY SATIN TRAIN WITH CLOUDS OF TRAILING TULLE MAY SIMPLY BE UNSUITABLE FOR A SMALL REGISTER OFFICE AFFAIR OR SECOND WEDDING.

△ THE TAILORED SUIT IS A FAVOURITE OPTION FOR MANY BRIDES, PARTICULARLY FOR REGISTER OFFICE AND SECOND WEDDINGS. THIS FIGURED SILK SUIT, DESIGNED BY GIANFRANCO FERRE FOR THE HOUSE OF CHRISTIAN DIOR, FEATURES AN ELONGATED JACKET WITH SHORT SLEEVES OVER A MATCHING SKIRT. A LARGE PICTURE HAT AND SHEER ORGANZA GLOVES COMPLETE THE BRIDAL OUTFIT.

The wide choice of venues that are available for marriage ceremonies today require that there be alternatives to the traditional, full-length white gown and veil. Modern couples are prepared to travel many miles in search of the perfect marriage location, which can often entail long-haul flights to exotic destinations. The desire to "do something different" has become a thriving business, with specialist companies and tour operators dedicating themselves to providing these services. Unfortunately for couples in the UK, at present, marriages may be celebrated only in religious buildings, town halls and register offices that are licensed. In other countries, the choice of marriage venues is far greater and ceremonies may be performed in places ranging from a beach or swimming pool to the top of a mountain, provided the vicar, minister or celebrant agrees.

THE PERFECT PLACE

A tropical island wedding ceremony is one of the most popular alternatives to the traditional church marriage. However, there is a wide variety of other popular locations for prospective brides and grooms. For example, the famous Chelsea Register Office in London's Kings Road, renowned as the location for rock stars' and media celebrities' weddings, is a popular venue for Americans and

Europeans who are attracted by its glamorous reputation.

The decision to marry somewhere other than a church can be made for a variety of reasons. Divorcees and couples who share different religious beliefs (as well as those without religious convictions) may be married at a register office. There are also those who decide to marry in unusual locations for all sorts of reasons – some incredibly romantic.

The availability of cheaper air travel to faraway places widens the choice of the location for the marriage ceremony. A couple may decide upon a deserted beach on some tropical island, where they will join hands beneath a gazebo decked with exotic flowers, or even aboard a cruise ship bound for a tropical isle. It is interesting to note that, while many Westerners are opting for weddings in exotic locations, large numbers of Japanese couples are arranging Western-style marriages after their own traditional ceremony at home.

Marrying in one's honeymoon destination is undoubtedly the ideal location for those whose vision of paradise is white sandy beaches and crystal blue waters and it can actually be less expensive than a large wedding reception at home. Favourite destinations are the Caribbean, the Virgin Islands, Jamaica and the Bahamas, while Kenya and the Far East are other options. All of these offer marriage facilities for non-residents. There are many travel operators who offer "wedding packages", where the hotel will provide champagne, cake and flowers, as well as the services of a clergyman or judge for the ceremony itself. Such holidays can be tailor-made to suit the bridal couple's wildest dreams, whether they be Kenyan safaris or trekking adventures in Vietnam. There are even special bridal exhibitions advertising weddings abroad and how to arrange one, complete with fashion shows and make-up and hairstyle demonstrations for hot climates.

Having arrived at their chosen resort, the bridal couple can choose to be married on the beach in daylight or at sunset, in a local chapel or in an exotic garden location. Most couples, however, have some idea of the ceremony location before their departure.

△ THE FARAWAY MARRIAGE, PERFORMED ON A TROPICAL BEACH IN THE CARIBBEAN, HAS BECOME ONE OF THE FASTEST-GROWING AREAS OF THE WEDDING BUSINESS. THE BRIDE HERE AT TAMARIND BEACH IN BARBADOS WEARS A BELOW-THE-KNEE 1920S-STYLE GOWN AND A HEAD-DRESS OF FRESH FLOWERS.

▷ A GOWN WITH A DETACHABLE TRAIN
IS A POPULAR REQUIREMENT OF MANY
BRIDES-TO-BE. LORENZO RIVA'S TRAIN
CAN BE REMOVED, LEAVING A SLENDER,
FULL-LENGTH EVENING GOWN OF HEAVY
LACE BEADED WITH PEARLS THAT CAN BE
WORN FOR A FORMAL EVENING
RECEPTION.

▽ FRAGILE WHITE LACE IS COMBINED WITH NATURAL HESSIAN IN LORENZO RIVA'S MODERN BRIDAL OUTFIT. THE BRIDAL BOUQUET, MADE OF FABRIC FLOWERS IS ALSO WRAPPED IN HESSIAN, WHILE THE TULLE VEIL IS EDGED IN MATCHING LACE.

△ AMERICAN DESIGNER ANNE KLEIN'S MODERN BRIDAL OUTFIT COMBINES THE TRADITIONAL VEIL AND TRAINED SKIRT IN A SOPHISTICATED TAILORED COAT WORN WITH CONTRASTING RED ACCESSORIES. A SIMPLE SHEAF OF TULIPS FORM THE BRIDAL BOUQUET.

△ A LARGE PICTURE HAT MAKES A SUITABLE ALTERNATIVE TO THE TRADITIONAL VEIL FOR A MODERN BRIDE. VALENTINO OF ITALY SWATHED THIS HAT IN LAYERS OF SILK TULLE, GIVING THE ILLUSION OF A VEIL.

▷ VIVIENNE WESTWOOD'S TWO-PIECE OUTFIT CONSISTING OF AN EIGHTEENTH CENTURY-STYLE CORSET AND MATCHING BRIEFS WOULD MAKE A NOVEL ALTERNATIVE TO THE TRADITIONAL WHITE WEDDING GOWN FOR A BEACHSIDE WEDDING CEREMONY. FRINGED ELBOW LENGTH GLOVES AND ANIMAL PRINT ACCESSORIES COMPLETE WESTWOOD'S CREATION.

▽ THIS WEDDING BIKINI BY DESIGNER KAREN ASHTON IS CLEARLY DESIGNED WITH THE TROPICAL WEDDING IN MIND. THE MATCHING HEADPIECE AND SCALLOP-EDGED TRAIN AND VEIL ARE BEADED WITH PEARLS, ECHOING THE DECORATION ON THE WHITE SATIN TWO-PIECE.

◁ WIDE-LEGGED PALAZZO PANTS AND
A TAILORED JACKET IN WHITE SILK MAKE
THIS TROUSER SUIT BY HERMÈS OF PARIS
A PERFECT MODERN ALTERNATIVE FOR
THE TROPICAL BRIDE. A LARGE HAT
WRAPPED IN TULLE AND A PLUMP POSY OF
RED AND WHITE FLOWERS TRANSFORM A
SUIT INTO A WEDDING OUTFIT.

▽ A PARASOL IS A PRACTICAL AS WELL
AS AN ATTRACTIVE ACCESSORY FOR A
FARAWAY WEDDING. FRENCH DESIGNER,
JEAN-PAUL GAULTIER, DRAPES SILK
TULLE OVER A COTTON PARASOL, GIVING
A MODERN ILLUSION OF THE
TRADITIONAL VEIL. THE BRIDE WEARS A
WHITE TROUSER SUIT.

▽ Sparkling diamanté, raw silk
and shimmering satin are used to
create the accessories for Dolce e
Gabbana's corset dress with net
skirt. The enormous belt buckle is
encrusted with pearls and
rhinestones while the handbag and
elbow-length gloves are of white
satin.

Elements of Modern Styles

Whatever the reason, for a non-church wedding, it is likely that
the bride-to-be who decides to "do something different" for her
marriage ceremony will also want to *wear* something less
conventional. Although a visit to most bridal salons may leave the
modern bride feeling that there are few alternatives to a traditional
gown, her choice is actually less restricted than it first appears.
Many bridalwear designers and manufacturers now include a
number of simple, shorter styles in their collections, while others
specialize exclusively in producing alternatives to the traditional
gown. The wedding outfits illustrated in this chapter have been
selected from a wide variety of sources. Some of them are created
by bridalwear designers and manufacturers, while others are from
the mainline collections of international *haute couturiers* and
fashion designers. Although the majority of these gowns are white
or ivory-coloured, there is no reason why a coloured outfit cannot
be worn. Many modern brides choose to get married in a colour
other than white.

Several factors may determine the bride-to-be's choice of gown.
If she feels that she will be uncomfortable in a full-skirted romantic
style, yet knows her mother has always dreamed of her floating up
the aisle in a cloud of white lace, she may choose one of the many
gowns available that have a detachable train or skirt. These
features are a popular requirement of many brides and appear on
both short and longer styles of gown. Bridalwear designer Juliet
Poyser maintains that comfort is a vital consideration when
deciding upon a wedding gown: "I think it is important to try and
echo a favourite dress or evening gown that the customer has
always felt fabulous in as well as comfortable. It is certainly worth
bearing in mind what its features were. It's no good if you try on a
dress, and you feel really restricted, or it's inappropriate for the
time of year". A bridal outfit could incorporate elements of a
favourite little black dress that has served its owner faithfully for
years; a smart suit could be translated into a luxurious fabric; or a
slender evening dress could be draped with a detachable train and

transformed for an evening reception.

A modern bride, for most people, is one clothed in a short dress or suit without the traditional trappings of veil, floral head-dress and cute bridesmaids trotting along behind her. Despite the disputes over hemlines that have dominated the editorial fashion pages of newspapers and magazines during the early part of the 1990s, the shorter skirt remains a popular choice for modern bridal gowns. While the fashion pundits continue to debate the demise of the short skirt, there are few signs of it disappearing completely. Most designers continue to present gowns of shorter lengths alongside longer styles. With regard to wedding gowns, every designer will stress the importance of accentuating the bride's best features. A bride-to-be whose greatest asset is her long, shapely legs, may well decide upon a short gown to emphasize them.

Fashion boutiques and high street clothing stores are a good source for shorter wedding outfits. Styles can be as understated or as daring as the bride-to-be chooses.

The short strapless gown, or straight slip dress, presents endless possibilities for the modern bride to create her own individual look. For the marriage ceremony itself, most brides choose to cover up bare shoulders, which are generally considered to be inappropriate in a church. Lengths of silk tulle or even crushed velvet wrapped around the shoulders as a stole and tied at the back can be left trailing to the floor as a train. A three-quarter length coat of sumptuous crushed velvet, in white or ivory, with a wide sash makes a luxurious cover-up for a winter bride. A short bolero jacket covers the shoulders without detracting from the shape of a slim-fitting gown.

A wedding gown is often, sadly, a prime example of conspicuous consumption as it is often worn only once. A gown made of the most luxurious materials and representing, representing the highest craftsmanship, yet usually worn for just one day, goes against modern ecologically aware thinking. This prompted Hollywood

▽ LAURA ASHLEY'S COTTON SATEEN SUIT FEATURES A PEPLUM JACKET WITH LEG O' MUTTON SLEEVES AND A SHORT STRAIGHT SKIRT. WORN WITH SILK FLOWERS IN THE HAIR AND A FORMAL BOUQUET, THIS OTHERWISE PLAIN SUIT WOULD APPEAL TO THE PRACTICAL BRIDE WHO WANTS TO BE ABLE TO WEAR HER WEDDING OUTFIT AGAIN.

bridalwear designer Susan Lane to create a range of Eco Dresses for her Country Elegance collection. The designer recycles plastic bubble wrap, paper doilies and plates as well as bottle caps in the gowns based on designs from her main collection.

A tailored coatdress is an elegant alternative to a dress or suit and many styles are inspired by the designs of 1950s couturiers, such as Christian Dior. The tailored shape of a coatdress, with a fitted bodice and long sleeves, is often balanced by a very full skirt worn over layers of stiff net. A large picture hat or smaller pillbox style and short gloves gives a 1950s feel to a coatdress outfit.

The bride's choice of wedding outfit will also be influenced greatly by her choice of location for the ceremony. A traditional gown *can* be worn at the local church or on the beach but this creates all kinds of practical difficulties. A silk or satin dress can be difficult to pack and a nightmare to iron on arrival, for example. To overcome this, a number of bridalwear companies now produce collections aimed exclusively at brides planning a tropical wedding. Berketex, a British bridalwear company, has a range called Affiniti that features short dresses with matching jackets and boleros as well as other styles with detachable trains. The more traditional, romantic-style gowns have appropriately shorter skirts, cut to ballerina-length to prevent them being damaged by trailing them through the sand. A cool cotton gown is ideal for a tropical wedding and also has the added attraction of costing considerably less than a pure silk or satin creations.

▽ THIS STRAPLESS SUNDRESS WITH MATCHING BOLERO BY AFFINITI COMES WITH A DETACHABLE NET OVERSKIRT THAT TRANSFORMS IT INTO A WEDDING GOWN THAT IS PERFECTLY SUITED TO A FARAWAY MARRIAGE. A SHORT VEIL OF WHITE NET IS WORN WITH THE WEDDING GOWN.

And now for something completely different...

Although most faraway wedding ceremonies are timed for the late afternoon to avoid the hottest part of the day, an adventurous bride might decide upon a white satin wedding bikini, beaded with pearls, for a beachside ceremony in the middle of the day. One such design, created by British designer Karen Ashton with the tropical island bride in mind, features a tulle train and matching veil beaded with pearls. A corset and matching briefs in silky white Lycra, featuring a gold print, complete with elbow-length white satin gloves, from Vivienne Westwood, could also be worn for a beach wedding. A practical bride (with a sense of humour) might opt for Ronald Joyce's plain white T-shirt printed in silver with the words "The Bride" and decorated with a silver bow. This costs less than a bottle of non-vintage French champagne.

Still on a practical note, a large hat or a decorative cotton parasol trimmed with lace are sensible accessories that will protect the bride from the sun if the marriage ceremony is to take place soon after arrival and before there has been any opportunity to work on a tan. As the Caribbean is prone to sudden rain showers a waterproof parasol should also be considered.

For a really exotic wedding outfit, the bride (and groom) could "go native" in their choice of attire. A grass skirt decked with flowers or a pareo, worn with or without a traditional bridal veil, would make a novel set of wedding photographs. Couples bound for Fiji (a popular destination for Australian weddings) may decide to get married in the traditional Fijian wedding costume of *tapa* cloth and *pandanus* leaves.

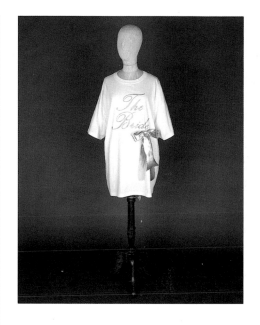

△ RONALD JOYCE'S COTTON T-SHIRT IS PRINTED WITH THE WORDS "THE BRIDE" IN SILVER ON THE FRONT AND "JUST MARRIED" ON THE BACK.

▷ LUCIANA DE STEFANO'S PRACTICAL WEDDING SUIT, CONSISTING OF A COLLARLESS TAILORED JACKET AND CITY SHORTS IN WHITE CRÊPE, IS DESIGNED TO HAVE AN AFTER LIFE, WHICH PRACTICAL BRIDES OFTEN DEMAND. THE SHORT WHITE LACE GLOVES AND SIMPLE SPRAY OF FLOWERS ARE EQUALLY UNDERSTATED.

▽ Siana's "Teapot dress" is cut to a princess line without a waistline and features a "lampshade" skirt. The ivory-coloured gown is trimmed in matching satin around the hem, sleeves and neckline, which is decorated with a large bow. The matching hat in ivory satin is also decorated with fabric bows.

◁ Unusual proportions create a dramatic effect in Sonia Rykiel's simple knitted skirt and skinny rib sweater worn with a diamanté-spangled veil. The bride wears white satin gauntlet gloves and carries a small posy of white flowers.

▽ GIVENCHY'S STRAPLESS GOWN
FEATURES A SPRAY OF LILIES-OF-THE-
VALLEY, A FAVOURITE WEDDING FLOWER,
WHICH DOMINATES THE FRONT OF THE
DRESS. AN ENORMOUS ORGANZA BOW
FORMS A TRAIN AT THE BACK.

▽ WEDDING SHOES CAN BE AS
TRADITIONAL OR AS AVANT-GARDE AS
THE STYLE OF THE WEDDING GOWN
ITSELF. HANNA GOLDMAN'S THIGH-
HIGH SATIN BOOTS ARE DECORATED WITH
RHINESTONES, WHILE A PAIR OF SILK
BROCADE LACE-UP SHOES ARE
ENCRUSTED WITH DIAMANTÉ AND GLASS
BEADS ON THE PLATFORM SOLES AND
AROUND THE ANKLE.

▷ METALLIZED ORGANZA FABRIC
EXTENDS UPWARDS TO FORM A SCULPTED
NECKPIECE ON ANDREW WILLIAM
BUCKLER'S SATIN LYCRA SHEATH GOWN,
GIVING A MODERN ILLUSION OF A VEIL.
THE PANELS OF ORGANZA ARE STIFFENED
WITH BONING AND FORM A CORSET
AROUND THE BODY.

▽ HAND-BEADED HAIR BOWS IN
PADDED SILK AND SATIN, COMPLETE
WITH MATCHING BEADED EARRINGS, BY
DESIGNER FLORENCIO MOGADO ARE AN
ATTRACTIVE ALTERNATIVE TO THE
TRADITIONAL WEDDING VEIL AND HEAD-
DRESS.

▷ THIS BEAD-ENCRUSTED BOLERO
JACKET BY AMERICAN DESIGNER BILL
BLASS CAN BE WORN OVER A STRAPLESS
WEDDING GOWN WHERE BARE
SHOULDERS FOR A CHURCH CEREMONY
MIGHT BE DEEMED INAPPROPRIATE. THE
JACKET IS MADE IN HEAVY GUIPURE
LACE, WITH CLUSTERS OF BEADS SEWN
ONTO THE FLORAL MOTIFS·

▷ LAYERS OF PRISTINE WHITE ORGANZA
ARE FASHIONED INTO A WRAPOVER COAT
BY ITALIAN DESIGNERS DOLCE E
GABBANA. THE ORGANZA IS USED TO
FORM AN ENORMOUS ROSE ATTACHED TO
THE WAISTBAND.

△ An organza trenchcoat makes a dramatic coverup for a strapless bridal gown. The design by Mirror Mirror, based on the classic male overcoat, is distinctly feminine. A bouquet of hot pink flowers with deep green foliage is carried by the bride.

▷ The classical Empire style is reinterpreted here by Dolce e Gabbana for a modern bridal gown. Layers of sheer chiffon are tied beneath the bust in a draped bow while opaque white hold-up stockings are visible beneath the miniskirt.

△ COUTURE OF THE 1950S IS THE
INSPIRATION BEHIND SIANA'S TAILORED
COATDRESS IN WHITE SATIN. THE SKIRT
IS STIFFENED WITH LAYERS OF WHITE NET
AND THE SHAWL COLLAR AND CUFFS ARE
FASHIONED FROM SHEER ORGANZA.

◁ A LOOSE CROCHET LACE MAXICOAT
IS WORN OVER WIDE-LEGGED LINEN
TROUSERS FOR DESIGNER MICHAEL KORS'
WOODSTOCK-INSPIRED WEDDING
OUTFIT, REFLECTING THE INFLUENCE OF
THE 1970S IN 1990S FASHION.

△ A TAILORED JACKET IN IVORY WOOL
IS WORN OVER A FRAGILE LACE SKIRT
WITH A LONG TRAIN FOR ROLAND
KLEIN'S COLONIAL-STYLE BRIDAL
OUTFIT. THE WEDDING HAT IS COVERED
IN LACE TO MATCH THE SKIRT AND
FEATURES A WIDE BRIM – A PRACTICAL
FEATURE FOR THE TROPICAL SUN.

OTHER OPTIONS

Brides-to-be looking for a simple alternative to the traditional full length gown to take abroad are often advised to choose one that is easy to pack. The wide variety of new fabrics, including microfibres, that simulate materials such as washed silk and require no ironing are a good choice for fluid shapes such as short slip dresses with flirty skirts. Fortuny-style pleated fabrics are perfect for packing as they actually need to be kept twisted when not worn to maintain the pleated effect. Cotton is obviously a good choice for a hot country and, when packed between layers of tissue, requires little ironing. A summer-weight suit consisting of a dress and jacket is also a popular choice for the bride bound for tropical climate and both items can, separately, form part of her holiday wardrobe after the marriage ceremony. Colonial-style outfits look particularly elegant on a tropical island bride.

ACCESSORIES IN THE TROPICS

Accessories for the tropical island marriage require careful consideration and should be practical as well as appropriate. A pair of very high-heeled court shoes, for example, will simply be comical if worn on a beach. A bridal bouquet and head-dress made of silk flowers can be purchased before the trip so that there is one less thing to worry about on arrival, although it is worth bearing in mind all the wonderful varieties of exotic flowers that will be available at the holiday destination as these can add to the effect beautifully. Indeed, most wedding packages include a bridal bouquet and a buttonhole as part of the service. Brides and grooms bound for Hawaii or Maui could consider wearing *leis* – the traditional floral wreath worn like a necklace.

The attractions of a detachable train have meant that it has become a feature of many bridal gowns. Not only does it free the bride from the responsibility of having to cope with yards of excess fabric at the wedding reception, but it also means that she can change her appearance without changing her dress.

5
FASHIONABLE
BRIDES

THE LONGSTANDING TRADITION OF SENDING A BRIDE DOWN
THE CATWALK AT THE END OF A FASHION SHOW IS AN
ESTABLISHED FEATURE OF BOTH *HAUTE COUTURE* AND
DESIGNER FASHION COLLECTIONS. FROM THE ROMANTIC AND
THE TRADITIONAL TO THE AVANT-GARDE AND EVEN
OUTRAGEOUS, THESE BRIDAL GOWNS REFLECT THE ESSENCE OR
THE INSPIRATION BEHIND THE DESIGNER'S COLLECTION.

▽ VALENTINO'S ROSE GARDEN BRIDAL
GOWN FEATURES A PUFFBALL SKIRT
DECORATED WITH SILK ROSES WORN
OVER A SILK TULLE UNDERSKIRT BOUND
WITH BANDS OF SATIN RIBBON. THE
PICTURE HAT IS ALSO SWATHED IN TULLE
AND ADORNED WITH SILK ROSES.

While some of the featured gowns might make a priest or vicar
blanch at the sight of them, others represent examples of
exquisite handwork on otherwise fairly traditional gowns.
Like Hollywood film producers, there is little that *haute
couturiers* like better than a society or
celebrity wedding as a publicity vehicle
for their bridal creations. Elizabeth
Taylor's eighth marriage, to Larry
Fortensky in 1991, saw the bride in a
yellow, ruffled gown by Rome-based
couturier, Valentino, while the beaded
outfit worn by the actress for her
reception was by Gianni Versace.
Australian businessman, Alan Bond's
daughter Susanne was married in a gown
by British designer Bruce Oldfield and
the large sum total of the wedding gown
and bridesmaids' outfits included the
cost of flights between London and
Sydney for fittings The dress worn by
Trudie Styler at her marriage to the
singer, Sting, was designed by Gianni
Versace at a reputed cost of $100 000.

Haute couture past and present

At the *haute couture* shows, unfettered by financial restraints and the commercial requirements of international buyers, these gowns are often sumptuous creations with several hundred hours of painstaking handwork having gone into their making. *Haute couture* is the pinnacle of the fashion industry, combining masterful cutting techniques with exquisite handwork, the best of fabrics and finish and the individual signature of the couturier. Indeed, it has often been said that many *couture* garments are so beautifully finished that they could be worn inside out.

Haute couturiers of the past are remembered for their particular style, which can also be seen to influence contemporary designers. The immaculate cutting and tailoring of a Balenciaga gown, for example, is highlighted by his characteristic elimination of detail. Madeleine Vionnet is credited with inventing the bias cut, which most people will recognize in the slinky evening gowns of the 1930s. Schiaparelli is famed for her painterly use of embroidery, witty detailing and her collaboration with artists such as Salvador Dali and Jean Cocteau. Coco Chanel gave women the little black dress and the jersey and tweed suits that have become staple items in many wardrobes. Christian Dior's New Look of 1947, with its sloping shoulders and very full skirts marked a dramatic change from wartime fashions. Dior's influence is evident in the full tulle skirts and tailored gowns that are popular bridal styles today.

The prices of *couture* gowns are prohibitive for the majority. According to fashion writer Lisa Armstrong, a *couture* gown might cost £20 000 / $31 000 (1990) and a wedding dress £100 000 / $155 000. In his book *The Fashion Conspiracy* (William Heinemann Ltd, London, 1988), writer Nicholas Coleridge describes the first $100 000 wedding dress. It was beaded by the famous Parisian company owned by François Lesage for an Arabian customer. Whatever the price, the designs of *haute couture* are a great source of inspiration.

△ A FULL NET TUTU SKIRT IS WORN WITH VIVIENNE WESTWOOD'S SHEER STRETCH LACE CORSET AND LEGGINGS. THE MODEL ALSO WEARS A PEARL CHOKER NECKLACE WITH A CAMEO DECORATION.

▽ MODEL CLAUDIA SCHIFFER WEARS
KARL LAGERFELD'S BODY-SKIMMING
BRIDAL GOWN FOR THE HOUSE OF
CHANEL. THE DESIGN FEATURES A SHEER
PANEL AT THE MIDRIFF STIFFENED WITH
BONING. THE BODICE AND TRAINED
SKIRT ARE MADE OF HEAVY FLORAL LACE,
WHICH IS ALSO USED TO EDGE THE
CIRCULAR-SHAPED VEIL.

△ SUMPTUOUS FABRICS AND COSTLY
TRIMMINGS FEATURE ON COUTURE
GOWNS – CHRISTIAN LACROIX DRAPES
LACE-TRIMMED TULLE EDGED WITH
PLEATED ORGANZA FROM THE SHOULDER
OF HIS GOLD CRINOLINE GOWN, HELD IN
PLACE WITH A SPRAY OF GOLD FLOWERS.

◁ JEAN-PAUL GAULTIER'S DESIGNER BRIDE WEARS AN ARAN-KNIT TUBE DRESS OVER LYCRA LEGGINGS AND BLACK LEATHER BIKER BOOTS. THE BRIDAL HEAD-DRESS IS MADE OF CURVED STEEL AND DECORATED WITH TRAILING TOILET ROLLS, WHILE THE BRIDAL BOUQUET OF DAISIES IS PINNED TO THE DRESS AS A BROOCH.

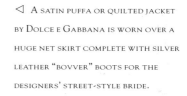

◁ A SATIN PUFFA OR QUILTED JACKET BY DOLCE E GABBANA IS WORN OVER A HUGE NET SKIRT COMPLETE WITH SILVER LEATHER "BOVVER" BOOTS FOR THE DESIGNERS' STREET-STYLE BRIDE.

▷ Calvin Klein's slender fishtail gown and completely plain veil, worn by model Christy Turlington, draws attention to the exquisite bouquet of lilies.

△ A French tradition of tying balloons to the bride's veil is incorporated into this design by Jean-Paul Gaultier for his catwalk show. The bride's outfit and the veil are made from plain cotton muslin.

△ MONTANA'S SATIN AND BEAD-
ENCRUSTED GOWN IS FRAMED BY THE
STIFFENED OVAL VEIL IN WHITE NET. THE
SKIRT OF THE GOWN IS MINI-LENGTH AT
THE FRONT AND DIPS DOWN TO FORM A
TRAIN AT THE BACK.

△ THIS PEACH-COLOURED DEVORE
VELVET GOWN BY RED OR DEAD
FEATURES A RUSSIAN BABUSHKA DOLL
PRINT. THE BRIDAL VEIL IS FASHIONED
FROM MANY LAYERS OF TULLE OF
DIFFERENT LENGTHS, GIVING A
WATERFALL EFFECT.

ACCESSORIZING DESIGNER GOWNS

As with all bridal attire, the gown itself is only part of the total look and accessories such as the head-dress and veil, shoes and bouquet require as much attention as the gown itself. The smallest details can make a simple outfit look spectacular and it is interesting to look at how designers accessorize their bridal creations. A slender fishtail gown by Calvin Klein is worn with the plainest veil, drawing attention to a beautiful bridal bouquet of white lilies. The inverted teardrop shape of the bouquet, in turn, echoes the simple lines of the gown. The oval shape of a veil by Montana is stiffened with wire, creating a stunning frame for the simple shape of his satin gown. A spray of frothy white tulle gives a waterfall effect to a bridal veil worn with a devore velvet gown featuring a print of Russian dolls by Red or Dead. British designer Jasper Conran pairs a plain, tailored jacket with a full tulle skirt and completes the outfit with a magnificent bridal head-dress.

▷ A MAGNIFICENT BRIDAL HEAD-DRESS
REPLACES THE TRADITIONAL VEIL AND
FORMS THE FOCAL POINT OF THIS
WEDDING SUIT BY JASPER CONRAN,
WHICH CONSISTS OF A TAILORED JACKET
AND A FULL SILK TULLE SKIRT.

EXAMPLES OF CONTEMPORARY COUTURE

The eclectic mix of *haute couture* and ready-to-wear designer bridal gowns featured in this chapter ranges from the traditional to the avant-garde. They have been selected from a vast number of *haute couture* and designer bridal creations that have graced the catwalks of international fashion over a number of years.

Paris couturier Christian Lacroix, whose house was established in 1987, is renowned for his theatrical use of colour, embroidery and decoration. Drawing inspiration from his native Provence as well as historical sources, his bridal creations are always rich and luxurious. As Lacroix writes in his colourful memoires *Pieces of a Pattern,* his clothes often combine inspirations from many diverse sources: ". . . wrought-iron work from Toledo, the austerity of Castille, the allure of Haile Selassie or the last Kings of Africa". His eighteenth century-style bridal gown modelled by his muse Marie Seznec features a boned bodice in cream silk with removable sleeves, attached by ribbon bows, and decorated with heavy gilt jewels at the front. The matching silk overskirt is ruched up on one side to reveal the quilted satin underskirt. The oval-shaped bridal veil features embroidered lace edges and the head-dress is a gilt tiara crown worn on top of the veil. The influence of Spain is clearly evident in Lacroix's black velvet bridal jacket with cornelli embroidery in white silk braid on the bodice and cuffs. The embroidery is carried through to the back of the jacket and is focused on a red velvet heart. A more recent bridal gown by Lacroix for his January 1993 couture show was modelled by Suzanne Aichinger, rumoured to be romantically linked with Prince Albert of Monaco, which attracted great publicity to the designer's creation for his show finale.

Karl Lagerfeld's arrival at the house of Chanel in 1983 caused great excitement in the fashion world. While some fashion purists denounce Lagerfeld's modern interpretations of this famous *couture* label as a travesty of Chanel's work, others welcome his often humorous reworking of the traditional Chanel image. The classic

▽ CHRISTIAN LACROIX'S MUSE MARIE SEZNEC MODELS HIS EXTRAVAGANT EIGHTEENTH CENTURY-STYLE GOWN IN IVORY SILK TAFFETA. THE BONED CORSET BODICE IS RICHLY ORNAMENTED WITH GOLD JEWELS AND ALSO FEATURES REMOVABLE SLEEVES THAT ARE TIED TO THE BODICE WITH RIBBONS. THE HEAVY LACE VEIL IS TOPPED WITH A BRIDAL

△ THIS BRIDAL OUTFIT, DESIGNED BY
KARL LAGERFELD FOR HIS FIRST
COLLECTION FOR THE HOUSE OF CHANEL
IN 1983, FEATURES A JACKET AND
CRINOLINE SKIRT OF SHEER ORGANDIE
TRIMMED WITH RUFFLES, IMITATING
CHANEL'S SIGNATURE USE OF BRAID
TRIM ON HER TWEED JACKETS.

hallmarks of the house of Chanel regularly feature in Lagerfeld's bridal outfits. The bridal gown for the first collection he designed for the house in 1983 consisted of a sheer organdie jacket and long, gathered skirt. The jacket was cut in the same shape as Coco Chanel's tweed ones and her famous braid edging was reworked by Lagerfeld as tiny ruffles of white organdie and these also trimmed the skirt flounces. A more recent Chanel bride wore a white bouclé tweed jacket, featuring the ubiquitous braid in navy and white, over a matching eighteenth century-style boned corset and enormous crinoline skirt. The bridal veil was fashioned from layers of lace ribbons topped with a miniature boater hat.

Italy's Gianni Versace is renowned for his use of exotic colours, extravagant beading and embroidery and richly printed textiles. One of his more famous wedding gowns was that worn by Baroness Francesca von Thyssen-Bornemisza at her marriage to Karl Hapsburg, grandson and heir to the last Austrian emperor. Her sumptuous bridal gown of white satin was a typical, though ornate, example of Versace's use of decoration on his designs. An example of Versace's style is featured here in which the long-sleeved bodice is completely covered in gold, black and silver beads and sequins, with silver, fan-shaped sequins around the neckline. The full skirt is also heavily embroidered with scrolls and flowers, while the scalloped hemline is echoed on the edge of the veil and this was outlined with sequins. The bridal bouquet is made of stiff gold hat net and a sequinned scroll motif is repeated on the white satin shoes.

The influences of other cultures are often incorporated into designs for bridal gowns, such as Gianfranco Ferre's Spanish infanta style for the house of Christian Dior in Paris. Fashioned in sumptuous metallic fabrics the gown was worn with a gold lace mantilla head-dress worn as a bridal veil. A white and silver gown that Karl Lagerfeld designed for a collection for Chanel featured Indian sari-style fabric for the full-skirted strapless gown. An interesting feature of this design was the veil, which forms part of the dress bodice.

Winter bridal gowns by couturiers often feature rich fur trims, such as Balmain's gown of snow-white satin that featured a high white fur collar reminiscent of those depicted in 1920s fashion illustrations. The overskirt was cut to form a deep train, trimmed with fur, over a short, pearl-encrusted underskirt. The bridal head-dress was a cloche-style hat embroidered with sequin leaves and pearls. Patou's trouser suit for a winter wedding featured a silk bustle train and a huge white fur hat. York and Cole's strapless silk gown with chiffon overskirt had separate fur "gloves" to match. Britain's former queen of punk, Vivienne Westwood, launched her first bridal collection for Liberty of London in January 1993. Although many a fashionable bride has incorporated one of Westwood's famous boned corsets into her wedding gown before now, this collection marked the designer's first official foray into the romantic world of wedding gowns. Westwood's "his and hers" gangster-style trouser suits in cream wool with giant satin lapels for the bride and groom came with matching top hats. The designer's teeteringly high rocking horse shoes for the bride and carpet slippers for the groom were created in shimmering white satin. Full-blown romantic gowns by Westwood featured boned corset bodices over skirts made of literally hundreds of layers of net with ribbons, while another full-skirted strapless gown in white organza was topped by a matching organza veil. Other designers who have turned to the romantic world of wedding gowns include Italy's design duo, Dolce & Gabbana. Realising that many customers were coming to them for white outfits from their mainline collection to wear as wedding gowns, the designers decided to produce a special wedding collection of 18 gowns which they launched in 1992. The gowns feature their signature boned bodices, with full skirts of tulle and silk decorated with pastel-coloured silk flowers. Accessories include flower chokers, bridal bags and shoes.

From Westwood's avant-garde bridal footwear to Christian Lacroix's sumptuous interpretations of the romantic wedding gown, the creations of *haute couturiers* and international fashion designers may be interpreted by the fashionable bride in many ways. She may fall for one designer's total look or, alternatively, she may simply be inspired by the way in which a designer attaches a veil to a head-dress or decorates a pair of shoes.

▽ THE INFLUENCE OF SPAIN AND BULLFIGHTERS' COSTUMES CAN BE SEEN IN LACROIX'S ORNATE BLACK VELVET BRIDAL JACKET, TRIMMED WITH WHITE SILK EMBROIDERY. THE PUFFBALL CRINOLINE SKIRT IS RUCHED AND GATHERED ONTO UNDERSKIRTS TO GIVE THE VERY FULL EFFECT.

▽ MODEL NAOMI CAMPBELL HERE
WEARS AN ORNATE SILVER AND GOLD
WEDDING GOWN BY ITALY'S GIANNI
VERSACE, WHICH FEATURES ORNATE
BEADING AND EMBROIDERY WORKED ALL
OVER THE DRESS. THE BRIDAL VEIL AND
SHOES ARE BOTH DECORATED WITH LACE
AND BEADED MOTIFS USED ON THE DRESS.

△ THIS MORE RECENT WEDDING OUTFIT
DESIGNED BY LAGERFELD FOR CHANEL IS
MODELLED BY CLAUDIA SCHIFFER. THE
CRINOLINE SKIRT, JACKET AND BONED
CORSET ARE FASHIONED IN OFF-WHITE
BOUCLÉ WOOL AND AGAIN FEATURE THE
CHARACTERISTIC BRAID EDGING.

△ RICH METALLIC FABRICS ARE USED
HERE BY GIANFRANCO FERRE FOR THE
HOUSE OF CHRISTIAN DIOR. THE BRIDAL
VEIL IS MADE OF GOLD TULLE TRIMMED
WITH HEAVY GOLD LACE.

▽ INDIAN SARI-STYLE EMBROIDERY IN
SILVER THREADS FEATURES ON THE SKIRT
AND "VEIL" OF KARL LAGERFELD'S
DESIGN FOR THE HOUSE OF CHANEL.
WHEN WORN DOWN, THE "VEIL"
BECOMES A SHAWL NECKLINE ON THE
STRAPLESS GOWN.

▷ THIS SHORT, OVAL-SHAPED VEIL WORN WITH DIOR'S GOLD BRIDAL GOWN IS TRIMMED WITH ORNATE WHITE LACE IN THE CENTRE AND AROUND THE EDGES, LEAVING THE BRIDE'S FACE COVERED WITH A LAYER OF TRANSPARENT TULLE.

◁ BALMAIN'S SNOW QUEEN BRIDE IS DRESSED IN WHITE SATIN TRIMMED WITH FUR, WHICH IS USED TO CREATE A HIGH NECKLINE AND FOLLOW THE LINE OF THE SKIRT TRAIN. THE BRIDE WEARS A BEADED CLOCHE-STYLE HAT.

▷ BALMAIN'S PEASANT-STYLE BRIDAL OUTFIT OF CRISP WHITE ORGANZA FEATURES PINTUCKED PLEATS ON THE SKIRT AND SHEER BALLOON-SHAPED SLEEVES. THE BODICE IS MADE FROM HEAVY COTTON LACE. A WHITE HEADSCARF TIED UNDER THE CHIN REPLACES THE TRADITIONAL VEIL.

▷ PATOU'S WOOL TROUSER SUIT
FEATURES A PUFFBALL SILK TRAIN
ATTACHED TO THE BACK OF THE
TROUSERS. A DEEP FUR HAT TRIMMED
WITH TAILS REPLACES THE VEIL IN THIS
WINTER BRIDAL OUTFIT.

△ YORK & COLE'S STRAPLESS GOWN
FEATURES A DRAPED CHIFFON OVERSKIRT
AND A SILK BROCADE BODICE. THE
BRIDAL OUTFIT IS COMPLETED WITH
SEPARATE FUR SLEEVES, GATHERED ONTO
SATIN BANDS.

◁ KENZO'S WINTER BRIDAL GOWN OF
IVORY SATIN IS TRIMMED WITH BANDS OF
CREAM FUR AND RICHLY EMBROIDERED
BRAID. THE FITTED TAILORED JACKET
HAS A POINTED PEPLUM FRILL AND THE
FULL SKIRT IS WORN OVER A CRINOLINE.
THE BRIDE WEARS A MATCHING FUR HAT.

▷ A SHEER LACE, BONED CORSET IS
WORN OVER A SHREDDED NET SKIRT WITH
LACE APRON SKIRT IN THIS DESIGN FROM
VIVIENNE WESTWOOD'S FIRST BRIDAL
COLLECTION FOR LIBERTY OF LONDON.

▽ VIVIENNE WESTWOOD'S GANGSTER-
STYLE MATCHING SUITS FOR THE BRIDE
AND GROOM ARE IN CREAM WOOL WITH
SATIN TRIMS. THE GROOM WEARS A
CREAM TOP HAT AND BOTH MODELS HAVE
WHITE SATIN WEDDING SHOES DESIGNED
BY WESTWOOD.

▷ DAVID EMANUEL'S PALE PINK BRIDAL
GOWN FEATURES A STRAIGHT SKIRT
WITH GATHERED OVERSKIRT. THE BRIDE
WEARS MATCHING PINK ACCESSORIES
SUCH AS THE SHORT GLOVES AND TULLE
VEIL WITH HEAD-DRESS.

6
FINISHING
TOUCHES

CHOOSING BRIDAL ATTENDANTS

THERE ARE VARIOUS TITLES GIVEN TO THE BRIDAL ATTENDANTS DEPENDING ON THEIR AGE AND SEX. ANGELA LANSBURY LISTS THE FOLLOWING IN HER BOOK *HOW TO BE A BRIDESMAID* (Sphere, London, 1983): CHIEF BRIDESMAID, MAID OF HONOUR, MATRON OF HONOUR, JUNIOR BRIDESMAID, RINGBEARER, FLOWER-GIRL OR FLOWER-BOY, PRESENTER OF LUCKY HORSESHOE AND BABY BRIDESMAID AS WELL AS BEST GIRL.

▽ OLDER BRIDESMAIDS USUALLY WEAR A SIMPLIFIED VERSION OF THE BRIDAL GOWN IN A PALE OR CONTRASTING COLOUR. ROSE & HUBBLE'S ANKLE-LENGTH DRESS IN RED MOIRÉ TAFFETA, ECHOES THE V-SHAPED BODICE AND FULL SKIRT OF THE IVORY SATIN WEDDING GOWN.

There are a wide variety of books available on wedding etiquette that deal with the various roles of each attendant and these are worth consulting before deciding on the attendants as particular roles call for particular skills. The chief bridesmaid (also known as the maid-of-honour in America) is referred to as the matron-of-honour if she is married. Usually a best friend or sister of the bride, the chief bridesmaid is to assist the bride while she dresses on the morning of the wedding and organize the younger bridesmaids. She is also responsible for helping to arrange the bride's dress, veil and train at the entrance to the church and throughout the day for the wedding photographs. The number of bridal attendants can vary from a single matron of honour to ten or more bridesmaids and page-boys and will depend on the size of the bride and groom's respective families, as well as their financial resources, as it is customary for the bride's father to pay for the attendants' outfits. What outfits the attendants are to wear is usually decided on by the bride, but if the bridesmaids are paying for their own dresses it is usual for them to have some say in the matter.

BRIDAL ATTENDANTS' CLOTHES

The outfits and accessories of the bridal attendants are often central to the theme and inspiration of a wedding. The colour and design of their clothes may echo the bride's gown, although, as author Angela Lansbury suggests, they might also be inspired by the surroundings and decor of the reception venue, which could be Victorian, Edwardian or even Art Deco. Whatever the inspiration behind the outfits and accessories for bridal attendants, their appearance needs careful thought and preparation if the finished result is to be successful.

Styles and colours of attendants' outfits vary enormously and can be as traditional or unconventional as the bridal gown itself. The most commonly worn styles, however, are usually based on historical designs and complement the bridal gown in some way, be it in colour, detail or shape.

The age of the attendants is an important consideration when deciding upon their outfits and if there is a wide difference in ages, it will probably be difficult to decide on how to dress all of them appropriately and harmoniously. While a diminutive flower-girl looks adorable in Victorian-style ruffles and matching bloomers, the prospect of being dressed in this way is likely to be a teenager's idea of a nightmare.

SOURCES OF ATTENDANTS' OUTFITS

Most bridal boutiques as well as individual dress designers will undertake to provide the attendants' outfits. These can be bought off-the-peg or designed and made to the bride's specifications, ensuring that they harmonize with the bridal attire. However, there are many other ways of choosing your attendants' outfits that will prove equally successful. Like the bridal gown itself, attendants' outfits can be bought from antique markets and thrift shops or made to the bride's own design by a nimble-fingered relative or the attendants' mothers. Alternatively, they can be hired from a fancy dress shop, a theatrical costumier or bought off-the-peg from a fashion boutique or department store.

△ DESIGNER ALLISON RODGER'S FLOWER-GIRL'S DRESS IN WHITE SILK DUPION FEATURES THE PANNIERED SKIRT DETAIL OF THE BRIDAL GOWN AND IS DECORATED WITH CLUSTERS OF FABRIC ROSES IN A DEEP, BURGUNDY-COLOURED VELVET.

▽ PIROUETTE'S SIMPLE BRIDESMAID'S DRESS IS MADE OF THE SAME FABRIC AS THE BRIDAL GOWN AND FEATURES A LACE-TRIMMED *FICHU* COLLAR. THE BRIDESMAID WEARS A FRESH FLOWER WRISTLET, WHICH IS AN EASY-TO-WEAR ALTERNATIVE TO A FLORAL BOUQUET, ESPECIALLY FOR YOUNGER ATTENDANTS.

▷ LUCIANA DE STEFANO'S ROSE PINK
GOWN FOR AN OLDER BRIDESMAID IS
ANKLE-LENGTH AND FEATURES LARGE,
PUFFED SLEEVES AND A BOW ON THE
BODICE. THE MODEL WEARS MATCHING
PINK GLOVES AND A PINK SILK FLORAL
HAIR DECORATION.

▽ OLDER BRIDESMAIDS AND YOUNG
FLOWER-GIRLS CAN BE DRESSED IN
COORDINATING OUTFITS TO SUIT THEIR
AGES. ROSE & HUBBLE'S PLAIN MOIRÉ
TAFFETA DRESS FEATURES SHORT, PUFFED
SLEEVES AND A V-SHAPED BODICE,
DESIGN FEATURES THAT ARE REPEATED
ON THE FLOWER-GIRL'S STRIPED DRESS
WITH A PLAIN CREAM UNDERSKIRT.

◁ ROSE & HUBBLE'S SHEPHERDESS
OUTFITS FOR FLOWER-GIRLS ARE MADE
FROM PRETTY PRINTED COTTONS, WITH
PUFFED SLEEVES AND PANNIERED SKIRTS.
THE FLOWER-GIRLS WEAR FRESH FLOWER
HAIR CIRCLETS, ECHOING THE COLOURS
IN THEIR DRESSES.

△ Tartan checked silks are a favourite choice for attendants' outfits. These dresses by Brides International combine off-white silk with black velvet and red tartan checks for summer weddings.

▷ Just Candy Confetti's ringbearer outfit in white silk is trimmed in rust-coloured silk to match the bridesmaid's dress. The child wears mid calf-length trousers and a waistcoat decorated with a large bow at the back.

△ THIS VICTORIAN DRESS FROM
THEATRICAL COSTUMIERS ANGEL &
BERMANS, FEATURES FULL, PUFFED
SLEEVES DECORATED WITH LACE AND A
HIGH-WAISTED BODICE. THE SKIRT HAS
ROWS OF PINTUCKS AND LACE INSERTS
AROUND THE HEM. THIS STYLE OF DRESS
IS A POPULAR CHOICE FOR YOUNG
BRIDESMAIDS AND FLOWER-GIRLS.

▷ THE FROCKCOAT WITH MATCHING
WAISTCOAT AND KNICKERBOCKERS BY
ANGEL & BERMANS IS A PLAINER
ALTERNATIVE TO THE HEAVY METALLIC
BROCADE OUTFIT. THE DEEP CUFFS ON
THE COAT ARE DECORATED WITH
COVERED BUTTONS.

WHAT STYLE?

The most obvious choice of style for attendants' outfits is that
which follows the same period style or design as the bride's gown.
For example, an off-the-shoulder gown with a full, gathered skirt
can be repeated in another colour for an older bridesmaid, while
younger flower-girls' dresses can feature the full skirt with a short-
sleeved bodice. A high-waisted Empire-style wedding gown can be
echoed in similar straight dresses for bridesmaids, without trains, in
pale colours such as rose pink, pale gold or in a darker colour for a
dramatic contrast. For younger attendants, the high waist can be
incorporated into a dress with a fuller, ballerina-length skirt and
tied with a broad ribbon sash, complete with flat satin ballet
slippers. Crisp organdie, which looks stunning with pintucks and
pleats as a feature on hemlines, can be used to great effect for
dresses of this style. Layers of muslin or embroidered Swiss lawn
create softer, more flowing dresses and look lovely worn over
matching pantaloons on little girls. Kate Greenaway outfits, so-
called because of the artist's drawings of children in Empire
costume, are perfect styles for young attendants to complement
a bride's Empire-style gown. Flower-girls' and bridesmaids' dresses can feature high waistlines and puffed
sleeves in floral or sprigged patterns on cotton, while
page-boys' outfits can echo the high waistline on
trousers that are buttoned to the shirt. This practical
yet decorative element is a good idea for
shirts will inevitably become untucked.

GROWN-UP BRIDESMAIDS
If the bridesmaids are all grown-up friends of the bride, their
gowns can be bought off-the-peg in a boutique or the fashion
department of a large store. In America, it is more usual to
have older bridesmaids and at a formal or semi-formal
evening wedding, they often wear evening gowns.
As previously mentioned, the trend for bridesmaids in the US to
wear black or black and white gowns has enjoyed widespread

popularity in America and looks particularly dramatic in wedding photographs. The American bridal magazine *Modern Brides* suggests floor-length, ballerina or knee-length dresses for bridesmaids at formal and semi-formal daytime weddings. According to New York-based designer Helen Morley, the trend for colour-themed weddings is also popular. This is when the female contingent of the wedding party wear a particular colour, which may be white or antique white to match the bride's gown. The less formal nature of English weddings, where the reception is usually held in the afternoon or early evening, means that older bridesmaids invariably wear ballerina-length or shorter dresses.

LITTLE BRIDESMAIDS

With younger bridesmaids and flower-girls, there is undoubtedly more scope for outfits than for older attendants, whose own personal preferences are usually taken into account. Little girls dressed in fairy outfits, ballerina-style net tutus and sailor dresses look most picturesque at a wedding.

Sailor suits and dresses are a very popular choice and so many bridalwear designers and manufacturers offer variations on this classic design. Sailor outfits for flower-girls and page-boys can be made in white cotton or even silk trimmed in navy or another contrasting colour, which are perfect for a summer wedding. For a winter wedding, sailor outfits can be made in heavier navy blue fabric with white trimmings. Sailor hats or straw boaters with matching bands are often worn instead of floral head-dresses.

A favourite style for young bridesmaids and flower-girls is the romantic Victorian dress with full skirt and puffed sleeves. Both Princess Diana and the Duchess of York chose this style for their female attendants at their respective royal weddings. The Princess of Wales' bridesmaids wore ivory silk trimmed with lace to match the bridal gown, while gold-coloured silk was introduced on the waist sashes and for the buckle-over satin shoes. Apricot silk, trimmed with lace and embroidered with seed pearls, was worn by the Duchess of York's bridesmaids. Both royals chose outfits for their page-boys to echo the military uniform worn by their grooms.

▽ LAYERS OF LAVISH LACE, SILK AND TULLE ARE USED TO CREATE THIS FLOWER-GIRL'S DRESS BY KESTERTON'S OF KNOWLE, ECHOING THE EXTRAVAGANCE OF *DANGEROUS LIAISONS*-STYLE BRIDAL GOWNS. THE HEAD-DRESS, BOUQUET AND DRESS DECORATIONS ARE MADE USING FRAGRANT DRIED FLOWERS.

The full-skirted dress, often featuring puffed sleeves, can be made in floral printed cottons for shepherdess-style outfits that can combine one or more different prints in layered overskirts. Plain silk bodices and puffed sleeves can be combined with skirts in layers of lace or tulle decorated with silk roses. Velvet or tartan silk are ideal for winter weddings and can look dramatic when combined in one dress.

RIDING HABIT STYLE

The riding habit-style gown translates well for outfits for bridesmaids and page-boys. Bridesmaids of all ages suit the tailored jackets of this style and an added attraction is that they can be worn again after the wedding. Chief bridesmaids and older girls can wear a simplified version of the bridal jacket in a contrasting colour or, perhaps, in a tartan patterned silk if this has been used to trim the bride's outfit. If the bride is wearing Victorian-style riding boots, the same style may be worn in fabric to match the bridesmaids' outfits. Younger flower-girls look most appealing in miniature versions of the riding habit style, complete with tiny top hats to match, while page-boy outfits can combine the tailored jacket with a pair of matching breeches and patent shoes with large buckles.

SOMETHING A BIT DIFFERENT

For more unusual outfits for young flower-girls and page-boys theatrical costumiers or fancy dress hire shops offer all kinds of possibilities. Fairy outfits and genuine ballerina tutus look perfect on little girls, complete with floral head-dresses and posies or hoops decorated with fresh flowers. These outlets are also a good source for period costumes.

▽ G. JOLLIFFE & CO'S NAVAL PAGE-BOY OUTFIT WAS STYLED ON THE OUTFITS WORN BY PAGES AT THE RECENT ROYAL WEDDINGS. THE PAGE WEARS A BOATER HAT AND FULL-LENGTH WHITE TROUSERS WITH THE WOOL JACKET.

PAGE-BOYS' OUTFITS

While the outfits of female attendants tend to echo the bride's
gown, those of page-boys can either reflect the groom's attire or
consist of the masculine style that goes with that of the
bridesmaids' dresses. If the groom wears a family tartan kilt, the
page-boys are often dressed in miniature versions of the Scots kilt
with all the trimmings. On a very small child, a waistcoat can be
worn on its own with a cotton lace-trimmed shirt instead of the
traditional "Prince Charlie" or montrose jacket. Scaled-down
morning suits, complete with waistcoats, cravats and top hats for
page-boys, can be bought or hired from mens' outfitters. Like adult
morning suits, these come in a choice of fabrics, with colours
ranging from pale grey to black and navy blue.

Another classic page-boy outfit is the Little Lord Fauntleroy suit,
inspired by the hero of Frances Hodgson Burnett's book of this
name. The Fauntleroy outfit consists of a velvet jacket
and knickerbocker trousers buttoned at the knees, a
white shirt with large lace collar and cuffs and silk
stockings worn with buckle shoes. Navy or black velvet
are traditional colours for Fauntleroy suits, although
lighter shades are more appropriate for spring or
summer weddings.

By tradition the ringbearer, who is usually a small
boy, wears all white, although his outfit can incorporate
colours to match those worn by the other attendants if
preferred. The ringbearer's cushion, onto which the
marriage band or bands are tied with ribbons, can be
made to match the bride's gown or the bridesmaids'
dresses. These cushions can be oval, round, square or
heart-shaped and most feature a strap underneath with
which they can be carried. The cushion may be
trimmed with lace or embroidered with beads, perhaps
with the initials of the bride and groom. A rich velvet
fabric is appropriate for winter weddings while a lighter
silk, in white or a pastel shade, is often seen
at summer weddings.

▽ IF THE BRIDEGROOM WEARS FULL
KILT DRESS, THE PAGE-BOYS ARE
INVARIABLY DRESSED IN THE SAME STYLE.
THIS MINIATURE OUTFIT BY G. JOLLIFFE
& CO FEATURES THE TRADITIONAL LACE-
FRILLED SHIRT WORN WITH A VELVET
WAISTCOAT, COMPLETE WITH SPORRAN.

◁ LYN LUNDIE'S FLOWER-GIRL DRESS
ECHOES THE LOW-WAISTED STYLES OF
THE 1920S. THE PRINTED CHIFFON DRESS
IS WORN WITH A MATCHING STRAW HAT,
DECORATED WITH SILK FLOWERS.

▷ CATHERINE BUCKLEY'S FLOWER-GIRL
DRESS IN LAYERS OF FRAGILE LACE
ECHOES THE 1920-STYLE BRIDAL GOWN.
THE CHILD'S DRESS IS BEADED WITH
ROWS OF TINY SEED PEARLS AND THE
HEAD-DRESS IS TWISTED FROM PADDED
SILK AND DECORATED WITH SPRIGS OF
GYPSOPHILIA. THE SATIN BALLET
SLIPPERS ARE HEAVILY FRILLED WITH
RUFFLES OF LACE.

◁ PLAIN DUCHESSE SATIN BRIDAL
SHOES BY DESIGNER EMMA HOPE FEATURE
A WIDE STRAP ACROSS THE INSTEP,
FASTENED WITH A SATIN BUCKLE. SHORT
WEDDING DRESSES OFTEN CALL FOR LESS
EXTRAVAGANT STYLES OF FOOTWEAR
THAT RELY ON SIMPLE, BEAUTIFUL
SHAPES AND FABRICS TO SPEAK
VOLUMES.

▷ SATIN BALLET SLIPPERS ARE A
POPULAR CHOICE OF FOOTWEAR FOR
YOUNG BRIDESMAIDS AND FLOWER-
GIRLS. DESIGNER WENDY WILLN
DECORATES A SATIN SLIPPER WITH
PEARLS AND SEQUINS TO ECHO THE
BRIDAL SHOES.

▽ THE LACE GARTER IS A TRADITIONAL
ITEM IN THE BRIDAL TROUSSEAU AND
USUALLY INCORPORATES "SOMETHING
BLUE" IN ACCORDANCE WITH THE OLD
RHYME. THIS BRIDAL GARTER IS TRIMMED
WITH BLUE RIBBON AND FABRIC
FLOWERS, DECORATED WITH TINY SEED
PEARLS.

▽ A SILK FLOWER CIRCLET DECORATED
WITH TINY APPLES MATCHES THE
FLOWERS ON ALLISON RODGER'S
FLOWER-GIRL DRESS OF WHITE SILK WITH
A TULLE OVERSKIRT.

BRIDAL BOUQUETS

Reference has been made throughout the book to the various types of bridal bouquets available that suit individual styles of wedding gowns. The flowers are as much a part of the traditional wedding as the white gown and tiered cake.

TRADITIONS AND SAYINGS

Like the bride's outfit, there are many customs or superstitions associated with flowers that brides often like to incorporate into the wedding theme. Perhaps the best known of these is that of the bride tossing her bouquet over her shoulder to the guests at the end of the wedding reception, the girl who catches it being the next to marry if the saying is true. Brides who wish to do this but also want to keep their bouquets as a memento of their wedding can have a replica made in fresh flowers. These can then be dried or some pressed and mounted in a picture. Also some florists will make a replica of a bouquet in silk flowers to keep after the wedding.

Orange blossoms are traditionally associated with weddings and are said to represent Juno's gift to Jupiter on their wedding day. Spanish brides often have a sprig of orange blossom sewn to their gowns as a symbol of good luck.

CHOOSING FLOWERS

It is advisable to seek the professional advice of a florist when choosing the flowers for a wedding as they will know what flowers are available at that time of year. Also, florists who specialize in wedding flowers and bouquets or regularly supply them will be able to offer guidance on what types of flowers and shapes of bouquet would best suit the wedding gown. It is therefore helpful to the florist to take along sketches and fabric swatches of the bridal gown and attendants' outfits so that flowers can be colourmatched.

SHAPES OF BOUQUETS

Fashions in the shapes of bridal bouquets fluctuate in the same way as do wedding gown styles. According to author Ann Monserrat, the grand shower bouquets of the 1890s remained fashionable for many years. They were superseded in the 1920s by a double-ended bouquet that was cradled in the crook of the arm.

Large round bouquets were popular during the 1940s and 1950s, while brides of the 1960s often carried small posies of flowers.

The huge formal cascade of white roses carried by Princess Diana in 1981, which reputedly took several florists a number of days to make, spurred this traditional bridal bouquet shape to popularity once more. However, while this type of bouquet is undoubtedly suited to the romantic gown worn by the Princess, there are many other styles that are equally attractive.

The most popular shapes of bouquet are the teardrop-shaped cascade, or shower of flowers, and the waterfall, both of which are best made by professional florists who are trained to wire the flowers, which is necessary when creating such structured shapes.

Posies, or nosegays as they were called by the Victorians, are usually rounded bunches of flowers with the stalks firmly held together at the centre back. The bunch can be backed with a piece of lace in the Victorian-style, framing the flowers beautifully, or tied with satin ribbons, these being left to hang as streamers.

Less formal bridal bouquets can be made from sheafs or bunches of flowers, simply finished with satin ribbon tying the stalks together. Lilies, tulips and other long-stemmed flowers are ideal choices for these simple styles.

It is worth while bearing in mind the attendants' ages when deciding upon the flowers they will carry at the wedding. As the *Illustrated London News* reported in 1923, "Small children are undoubtedly the most ornamental attendants for the bride . . . (but) they have the unfortunate knack of either dropping their bouquets altogether . . . or of letting slip some

▽ BIDDULPH & BANHAM'S WINTER BRIDE WEARS A VEIL OF RED NET WITH A CROWN HEAD-DRESS DECORATED WITH RED ROSES. THE BRIDE CARRIES A SEASONAL BOUQUET OF DELICATE FERNS AND WINTER ROSES.

of the flowers. Practical fashion has surmounted the difficulty by introducing the bridesmaid's basket."

Long-handled baskets, filled with fresh flowers or hoops entwined with blooms and greenery, are much easier for small hands to grasp without dropping them somewhere down the aisle. Floral pompons, which are balls of flowers suspended from a satin loop of ribbon are also easy for little ones to carry. Fresh flowers tied to one wrist is another pretty idea for younger bridesmaids. A small spray of flowers can be attached to a band of ribbon or Velcro. Also, prayerbooks can be decorated with a spray of fresh flowers and long silk ribbons and make an appropriate alternative to a bouquet or posy. Buttonholes, or boutonnieres, are optional for small page-boys and can match those worn by the groom, best man and ushers.

The flowers chosen for flower baskets, posies, nosegays, hoops or whatever can be echoed in fresh flower head-dresses for bridesmaids and flower-girls. These can range from the simplest option of a perfect bloom held in the hair by means of a haircomb or grip to a full circlet of leaves and blooms. Evergreen leaves and berries are striking alternatives to flowers for winter weddings and can be used to create head-dresses and bouquets trimmed with red and green ribbons.

OTHER FLOWERS

. . . .

While male members of the wedding party usually wear carnations in their buttonholes, either with or without greenery, alternatives include using one or more of the same flowers used in the bridal bouquet, extending the colour theme of the wedding. Corsages, too, worn by the bride and bridegroom's mothers, can incorporate these flowers.

Dried or silk flowers are a popular option for many brides and their attendants as they can be guaranteed not to wilt during the day and can be kept afterwards. There are many firms specializing in bridal accessories made from silk flowers, dried leaves and flowers and even fruit and vegetables, which can make stunning arrangements.

◁ GIANFRANCO FERRE'S BRIDE CARRIES
A BOUQUET OF TRAILING IVY LEAVES
SPRAYED GOLD, WHICH ECHOES THE
LUXURIOUS METALLIC FABRICS USED IN
THE WEDDING GOWN.

▽ ORANGE, YELLOW AND RED ROSES ARE COMBINED WITH TRAILING IVY IN A SMALL CASCADE BOUQUET. THE BRIDAL HEAD-DRESS CONSISTS OF A CLUSTER OF ORANGE ROSES, HOLDING THE SCALLOP-EDGED VEIL IN PLACE.

▷ A PLUMP, ROUNDED BOUQUET OF WHITE ROSES BACKED WITH LAUREL LEAVES, IS CARRIED BY VIVIENNE WESTWOOD'S MUSE MODEL SARAH STOCKBRIDGE. THE DEEP GREEN FOLIAGE SETS OFF THE DRAMATIC BRIDAL GOWN OF PLAIN WHITE ORGANZA.

△ BRILLIANT YELLOW ROSES ARE USED TO CREATE THIS BRIDAL BOUQUET AND HEAD-DRESS, WORN WITH PRONUPTIA'S ORNATELY BEADED SATIN WEDDING GOWN.

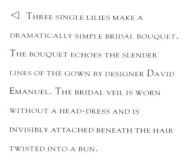

◁ Three single lilies make a dramatically simple bridal bouquet. The bouquet echoes the slender lines of the gown by designer David Emanuel. The bridal veil is worn without a head-dress and is invisibly attached beneath the hair twisted into a bun.

SPECIAL LINGERIE

Most brides dream of wearing luxurious silk underwear on their wedding day and the wired lace basque is perhaps the most coveted item in a bride's underwear trousseau. Complete with lace-trimmed stockings and the traditional bridal garter, these items can be quite expensive, so should be given careful thought.

When buying underwear for the wedding day, the design of the gown should be taken into consideration. There are companies who specialize in bridal corsetry and lingerie, such as low-back corsets and bustiers. The ultimate indulgence is made-to-measure wedding lingerie. This can be very expensive and, unless the bride has special requirements, should be unnecessary as most boutiques offer excellent ranges of ready-to-wear lingerie collections.

Plunging necklines require special bras, while a slim-fitting sheath dress will require underwear that will give smooth curves to the figure, so suspender belts and lace bras, which often create little lumps and bumps beneath a fine fabric will not be suitable.

Some bridal gowns require little extra support. Boned bodices, for example, have excellent shaping already built in, so a bra is usually optional.

As many wedding gowns are chosen without consideration to the time of year, thermal or silk and wool mix underwear can be a good choice for the winter bride. Despite the rather unromantic connotations, some very pretty styles of thermal underwear are available, trimmed with delicate lace in both white and soft pastel colours. A petticoat with a net "bustle" at the back of it is a good style to wear

▽ LAURA ASHLEY'S NET PETTICOAT FEATURES A COTTON BASQUE, WITH THE FULLNESS OF THE NET FALLING FROM THE HIPLINE. THIS STYLE IS PARTICULARLY FLATTERING AS IT PREVENTS UNWANTED BULK AT THE WAISTLINE.

beneath a gown featuring a train. Petticoats and net underskirts give added fullness to skirts and also provide extra layers beneath fine silks that will otherwise be somewhat transparent in bright daylight. Jill Thomas, author of *The Complete Wedding Book* (Wardhook, London, 1991), maintains that petticoats are essential for both brides and bridesmaids. She recalls one wedding that she attended where the bride was photographed in her crinoline gown with the sun behind her and that, ". . . when the photographs came out she was standing naked with a cage around her". This is worth bearing in mind when choosing fine silks and satins for a bridal gown and those of attendants.

There are many hosiery companies that produce special tights and stockings for brides, featuring motifs such as hearts, wedding bells and horseshoes on the ankle or decorated with rows or pearls or diamanté. Whether sheer or opaque hosiery is chosen will usually be determined by the design of the dress. A full-skirted *Dangerous Liaisons*-style gown suits white or ivory opaque legs as only a glimpse of ankle will usually be seen. A short, or knee-length gown, though, looks better with sheer hosiery as a solid block of a pale colour can be very unflattering. Whether tights or stockings are worn is a matter of personal taste, although many brides choose stockings as these can be worn with the traditional bride's garter. The bridal garter is often blue or decorated with a blue ribbon to add the blue element of the "Something old, something new . . ." proverb to the bride's ensemble.

△ This classic bridal basque by Gossard is worn with designer Lyn Lundie's short gown of ivory silk with a detachable train.

▷ Delicate lace-trimmed stockings are worn under designer Christian Lacroix's full, embroidered, lace skirt. This pretty style of "hold-up" hosiery can be worn with full-length gowns and eliminates the need for a suspender belt.

▷ THIS PAIR OF RED SILK WEDDING
SHOES BY DESIGNER EMMA HOPE FEATURE
WHITE SILK APPLIQUÉ LOVEHEARTS
ENTWINED BY CHERUBS WITH WINGS AND
GLISTENING HAIR EMBROIDERED USING
GOLD GLASS BEADS.

▽ ROMANTIC-STYLE BRIDAL SHOES BY
CRISTINA MAKE IDEAL FOOTWEAR FOR
FULL-SKIRTED WEDDING GOWNS. THE
CREAM SILK SHOE FEATURES A SILK
ROSETTE DECORATED WITH A PEARL
CENTRE, WHILE THE PALE PINK SILK STYLE
FEATURES A BOW WRAPPED OVER THE
FRONT OF THE SHOE SEWN WITH PEARLS.

▷ RINGBEARER CUSHIONS BY
KESTERTON'S OF KNOWLE COME IN RICH
RED VELVET TRIMMED WITH LACE AND
FRAGRANT DRIED ROSES FOR WINTER
WEDDINGS OR EMBROIDERED SILK
TRIMMED WITH IVORY BOWS AND LACE
FOR SUMMER WEDDINGS.

A FINAL NOTE

Whether or not she decides to have a full-blown traditional wedding, complete with all the trimmings, or opt for an exotic ceremony on a tropical beach, every bride-to-be wants the wedding to be perfect in every way. The choice of gown, accessories and outfits for the attendants will be important parts of wedding plans. Although the details can be time-consuming and at times frustrating to organize, the end result is always worth while and will be captured forever in those treasured wedding photographs.

Most Western-style weddings will include a white gown, a tiered cake and an abundance of flowers, but no two weddings are identical. From the coloured sash on a flower-girl's frock, echoed in the ribbons decorating the wedding cake, to a love heart painstakingly embroidered on the toe of a silk shoe, every detail bears the stamp of the couple's individual style and personality, making *their* wedding different to everybody else's

It is hoped that this book will provide ideas and inspiration that can be drawn upon to make your wedding day a truly memorable occasion.

◁ THIS IS A SELECTION OF BRIDAL GIFTS FROM KESTERTON'S OF KNOWLE. THE SILK TEDDY BEAR IS OFTEN GIVEN TO A SMALL CHILD TO CARRY RATHER THAN A BOUQUET. THE SILK BALLET SLIPPER, DECORATED WITH DRIED ROSES AND LACE, IS A GOOD LUCK MEMENTO. THE BASKET IS FILLED WITH POT POURRI BAGS, WHICH ARE AN UNUSUAL ALTERNATIVE TO BAGS OF SUGARED ALMONDS (CONFETTI) GIVEN TO WEDDING GUESTS.

INDEX

ACKNOWLEDGEMENTS

QUINTET PUBLISHING WOULD LIKE TO THANK THE FOLLOWING FASHION HOUSES, DESIGNERS AND PHOTOGRAPHERS FOR THEIR PERMISSION TO REPRODUCE COPYRIGHT MATERIAL. WHILE EVERY EFFORT HAS BEEN MADE TO TRACE COPYRIGHT HOLDERS, THE PUBLISHER WOULD LIKE TO APOLOGIZE SHOULD ANY OMISSIONS HAVE BEEN MADE.

t = top, b = bottom, l = left, r = right, c = centre, f = far, m = middle

p6 photograph by Brendan Beirne; p7 Lorenzo Riva, Italy; 8 Lorenzo Riva, Italy; 10 B. T. Batsford Ltd; 11 t Hulton Deutsch Collection, b Catherine Buckley; 12 t photograph by Brian Aris, b Robert Wilkinson; 13 l photograph by Niall McInerney, r Lorenzo Riva, Italy; 14 photograph by Mike Jones; 15 Ronald Joyce (London) Ltd; 16, 17 Angel & Bermans (Theatrical Costumiers); 18 l Luciana de Stefano, r Deborah Milner; 19 Niall McInerney; 20 Cecilia; 21 BT Batsford Ltd; 22 Niall McInerney; 23 Lazaro for Riccio, New York; 24 t Florencio Mogado, m Designed by Hanna Holdman, photograph by T Hurst, b Florencio Mogado; 25 Lorenzo Riva, Italy; 26 Chapeaux Carine, New York, photograph by Joel Greenberg; 28 l Niall McInerney, r Dress by Zandra Rhodes, photograph by Koo Stark; 29 photograph by Mike Owen; 31 Brendan Beirne; 32 l Andrea Wilkin, r Watters & Watters; 35 Dress by Edith Reilly, Twentieth Century Frocks; 36 l Catherine Buckley, photograph by Christine Thery, r Lyn Lundie Ltd; 37 l Brides International, r Designed by Caroline Amato, photograph by Daniel Mondavian; 40 Lyn Lundie Ltd; 41 Andrea Wilkin; 42, 43 Angel & Bermans; 44 t Laura Ashley, l Gina Shoes, Knightsbridge, r Yvonne Damant; 45 Niall McInerney; 46 Brendan Beirne; 47 l Designed by Catherine Davighi, r Allison Blake, London; 48 Brendan Beirne; 49 t Yumi Katsura, 1992 Spring Collection in Barcelona, b Lorenzo Riva, Italy; 50 l Philippa Lepley, photograph Rollo Snook, r Brides International; 52 Niall McInerney; 53 Ronald Joyce (London) Ltd; 54 tl Victor Edelstein, tr Ben Yeung, Kensington, London, b Miss Jenny, Italy; 55 Stevie's Gowns; 56 Hulton Deutsch Collection; 57 Rapsimo, Australia; 58 Alfred Angelo; 59 Van Lear Bridals, New York; 60 t Pronuptia, "Louise", b Designed by Catherine Davighi, "Rose-Marie" 61 The Wizard of Gos; 62 l Niall McInerney, r Silk; 63 Shoes by Peter Fox, New York; 64 t Droopy & Brown's by Angela Holmes, photograph by Crickmay, b Angel & Bermans; 65 t photograph by Mike Owen, b Niall McInerney; 66 Brendan Beirne; 67 Niall McInerney; 68 Donna Salado; 69 l Droopy & Brown's by Angela Holmes, photograph by Crickmay, r Niall McInerney; 70 l Shoes by Peter Fox, New York, r Brendan Beirne; 71 Niall McInerney; 73 Tamarind Beach, St James Beach Hotel; 74 Lorenzo Riva, Italy; 75 l Lorenzo Riva, Italy, t + r Niall McInerney; 76 l Brendan Beirne, r Niall McInerney; 77 Niall McInerney; 78 Niall McInerney; 79 Laura Ashley; 80 Brides International; 81 t Ronald Joyce (London) Ltd, b Lucian de Stefano, Italy; 82 l Niall McInerney, r Brendan Beirne; 83 l Niall McInerney, r Designed by Hanna Goldman, photograph by T Hurst; 84 l Florencio Mogado, t Andrew William Buckler, b Niall McInerney; 85 Niall McInerney; 86 l Brendan Beirne, r Niall McInerney; 87 l Niall McInerney, r Brendan Beirne; 88 Roland Klein; 90–94 Niall McInerney; 95 l Niall McInerney, r Red or Dead; 96 Jasper Conran; 97–103 Niall McInerney; 104 t + l Brendan Beirne, br David Emanuel Couture, made by appointment only; 106 Rose & Hubble (dress patterns by Butterick); 107 t Brendan Beirne, b Dresses by Pirouette, photograph by M Burton-Pye; 108 t Luciano de Stefano, bl + br Rose & Hubble (dress patterns by Butterick); 109 t Brides International, b Brendan Beirne 110 Angel & Bermans; 111 Kesterton's of Knowle; 112 G Jolliffe & Co; 113 G Jolliffe & Co; 114 Lyn Lundie Ltd; 115 t Catherine Buckley, bl Emma Hope Shoes, br Christina and Wendy Willn shoes; 116 t Lucky Legs, b Brendan Beirne; 117 Brendan Beirne; 118 Niall McInerney; 120 l Ronald Joyce (London) Ltd, tr Pronuptia, "Celia", br Brendan Beirne; 121 David Emanuel Couture, made by appointment only; 122 Laura Ashley; 123 t Lyn Lundie Ltd, b Niall McInerney; 124 tr Emma Hope Shoes, l Cristina shoes, b Kesterton's of Knowle; 125 Kesterton's of Knowle. Angel & Bermans garments and additional shoe photography by Martin Norris.